CAROLINA EARLY LEARNING ACTIVITIES

Book Two

David L. Lillie

Timothy M. Sturm

illustrated by
Patricia Collins

Walker and Company
New York

Editorial Revisions by Barbara Christesen
Illustrations by Patricia Collins
Mary Kalbach Horan, Production Editor

The activities in this book are selected and adapted from the *Carolina Developmental Curriculum Book One: Activities in Gross Motor, Fine Motor, and Visual Perception*, Timothy M. Sturm, editor, Susanne Creasey, Gloria Harbin, Susan Holt-Helmer, Tim Sturm, and Claire Weaver, contributors; *Book Two: Activities in Reasoning, Receptive Language, and Expressive Language*, Timothy M. Sturm, editor, Tom Clark, Susanne Creasey, Gloria Harbin, Linda Rand, and Tim Sturm, contributors; and *Book Three: Activities in Social Emotional Development*, by David L. Lillie, Ann L. Forman, and Beth McCabe.

First published in the United States of America in 1987 by the Walker Publishing Company, Inc.
Typography by Universal Printing and Publishing Company, Inc., Chapel Hill, North Carolina

ISBN: 0-8027-9327-4

Printed in the United States of America

10 9 8 7 6 5 4 3 2 1

Cover Design by Jeannie Friedman, Design Five.

CONTENTS

INTRODUCTION

The *Carolina Early Learning Activities* is a two-book set of games, crafts, and other learning activities for preschool and kindergarten.

Book One contains 176 activities to develop the skills that three- and four-year-olds need in order to be ready for kindergarten and the grades.

Book Two offers 168 activities that will help four- and five-year-olds make smooth transitions from the play-oriented environment of preschool to the more demanding first-grade classroom.

Many teachers of five-year-olds will find it helpful to use some activities from Book One for children who need review or extra help. Many preschool teachers, on the other hand, will have some children who are ready for kindergarten-level tasks. These teachers will find Book Two a useful supplement to their inventory of learning experiences.

Both books are designed to give youngsters the support and preparation they need for success in the primary grades. The activities have been thoroughly evaluated in terms of their appropriateness for, and effectiveness with, three-, four- and five-year-olds.

The Activities

At the top of each lesson page, a purpose statement (e.g., "to learn to share") tells the teacher the primary goal of that activity. This statement makes it easy to locate activities that will serve the instructional interests of the class from day to day.

Although the lessons are designed for use in groups of three to seven children, many of the exercises can be used with a larger group or the whole class. The teacher or aide presents each activity to the children and then helps with any problems along the way. It is important that an atmosphere of fun and excitement be maintained throughout all the activities. Young children lack the attention spans necessary for learning in a formal atmosphere.

For almost every lesson, there are two *follow-up activities* that the teacher can allow small groups or pairs of children to work on. The tasks are designed to give children extra work on the skills taught in the larger group and allow them opportunities to apply their newfound knowledge in a variety of situations—while freeing the teacher to help other youngsters who may need assistance.

In almost all cases, the teacher should feel free to alter activities to better suit the childrens' needs. In many cases, several activities have been provided to teach the same skill. For example, two games are offered to help children practice the large-motor skill of skipping (Knee-High Jump and Follow the Yellow Brick Road). The variety of activities offered to teach a single skill allows the teacher the flexibility to choose the best approach for her class, or all approaches if she feels various experiences are necessary.

The Seven Areas

There are activities in this book for seven learning areas:

- large motor skills
- small motor skills
- visual skills
- reasoning
- listening skills
- language skills
- social-emotional development

In general, the activities for each area move from easy to more demanding. For example, in small-motor learning, children are taught to place and remove large pegs in a pegboard, using both hands simultaneously (Two by Two), before they are asked to fold a square of paper into a triangle to create animal figures. Working first with real objects smooths the way for later work with pencil and paper.

The teacher should use judgment in choosing activities. Ideally, two or three activities from each of the seven areas should be presented each week. Whether or not the activities are used in the order they follow in this book is up to the teacher. Who knows better the needs and abilities of the youngsters in the class?

Frequently, while there is one primary purpose in each activity (e.g., the small-motor activity Popsicle Stick Frames), several skill areas are often touched on when the activity is presented. When children learn to make simple square frames out of popsicle sticks, they are not only perfecting a small-motor skill—they are also learning:

1. to share (social-emotional skills),
2. to follow directions (listening skills), and
3. to perform other small motor tasks (pasting, coloring, taping).

The teacher should view each and every lesson in terms of its potential to speed development of the whole child.

Grouping

Most early childhood classrooms use various grouping methods to help children master skills.

Large groups. In most schools—at the beginning of the day and several times thereafter—all children are brought together into one or several large groups (depending on the number of adults). In the large group, they are introduced to concepts that they will work on later in small groups or individually. The large group is also the natural setting for teaching listening skills (storytelling, etc.) and music, and for playing large-motor games.

In general, large-group activity should separate periods of small-group work and should come before introducing children to new tasks. Large groups are for seven or more children.

Small groups. These groups allow the teacher to individualize instruction. In a large group, the teacher will often observe that children have widely varying skill abilities. The small group allows children of like ability to come together and work on a specific task. Both large- and small-group work require a teacher, aide, or other adult's presence since the children need special guidance and/or immediate feedback on their performance. A small group consists of six or fewer children and one adult.

Working in pairs. Many activities may be effectively used by two children working together quietly—sharing the task and discussing it.

Independent work. In some situations, the teacher can give a child a specific assignment to work on alone. If the child is having trouble crumpling paper into balls, for example, and all the other children have mastered that task—the teacher may give the child a special activity (such as modeling clay into balls) to work on alone.

Free play. Often, after children have had to focus on a particularly demanding activity or when they have mastered the work the teacher is helping others with, they should be allowed to choose a toy (a pile of wooden blocks, the sand table, etc.) to play with on their own. For free play and independent work, it is helpful to establish the following rules.

1. Children must remain in their chosen areas as long as others are in group work.
2. Children must play quietly and appropriately.
3. Children may not interfere with other groups.

It is best to have not more than two small groups in independent or free play at one time. To do so is to invite disruptions. It is also important to limit the duration of these periods. Small children have short attention spans which often seem to improve only with growing older rather than through practice!

Classroom Arrangement

The way you should organize the space in your classroom depends on a number of things. The most important question to ask is: What kinds of interest areas do I need for small-group work? To some extent, the answer to this question lies in knowing the activities you plan to use and the materials you will have on hand. The following list includes most of the common interest-center designations.

KINDS OF INTEREST CENTERS

Arts and Crafts (for small motor, social/emotional, language)
Blocks (for reasoning, social/emotional, and small- and large-motor)
Cooking (all skills)
Science and Nature (all skills)
Homemaking or Dramatic Play (for language, social/emotional)
Books or Listening (for language and listening)
Music and Movement (for large and small motor, listening, language, social/emotional)
Table Games (for reasoning, social/emotional)
Water Table (for social/emotional, language)
Sand Table (for social/emotional, language)

Of course, you can always designate one area of your classroom as a "changing center"—one that you alter as the interests and needs of the children develop over the course of the year.

Most classrooms do not have or need all of the centers in this list, and the ones they have at the beginning of the school year are often changed by the end.

The location of the interest centers in the classroom depends upon the following items.

Things to Consider When Locating an Interest Center

Carpeting (important for blocks and floor work)
Tile (important where children work with liquids)
Electrical Outlets (needed in kitchen, music center, etc.)
Water Source (important for water table, art, cooking, science)
Tables (needed for games, art, nature and science)
Light Sources
Kitchen
Space for Eating and Sleeping
Restrooms
Exits

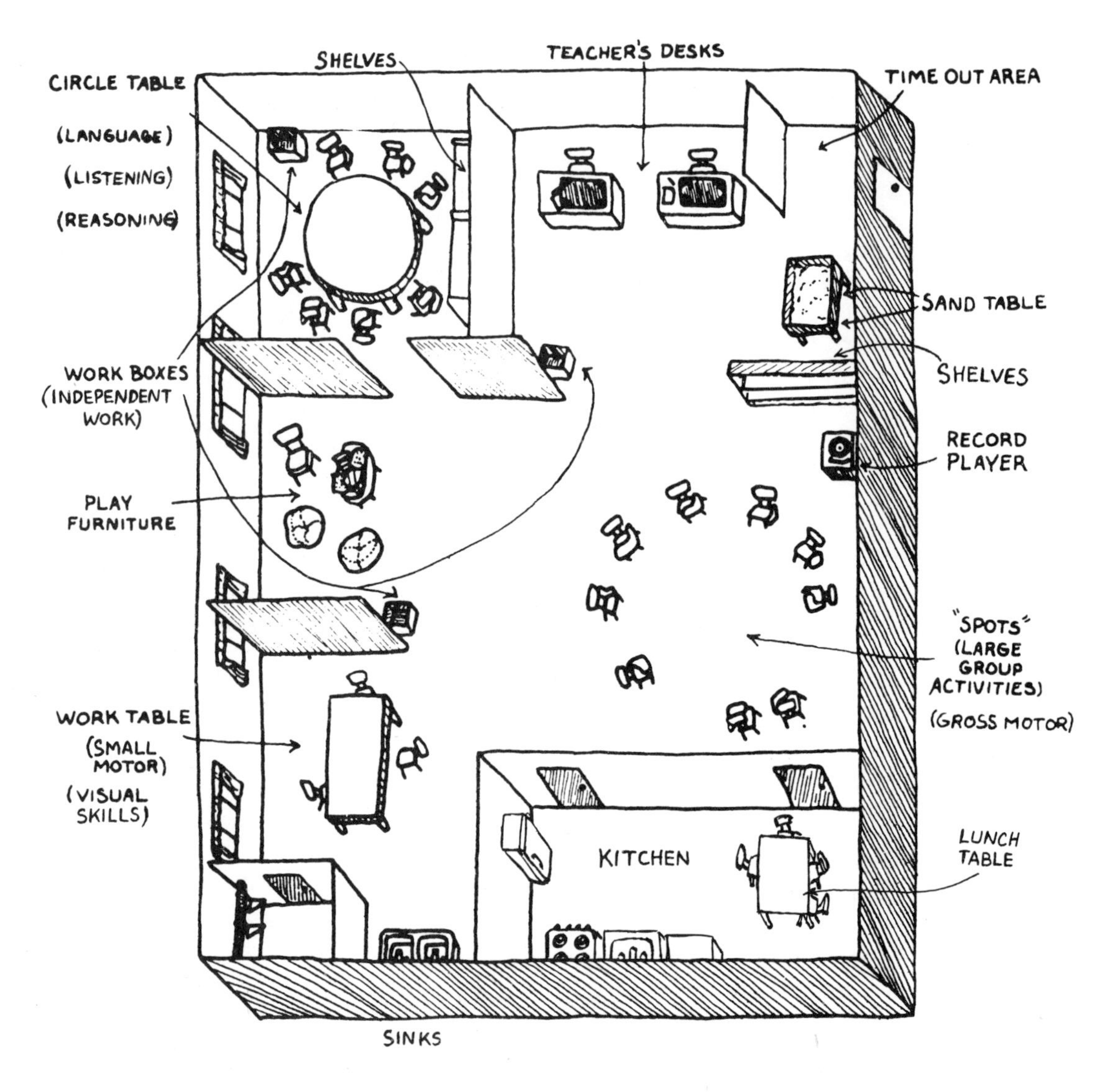

FIGURE 1: SAMPLE CLASSROOM

As you set up the centers, keep in mind

1. that large-group activities require the most space,
2. that centers requiring some of the same materials should be close together (e.g., language, dramatic play),
3. that centers that involve quiet activities should be close together (e.g., table games, books, etc.)
4. that centers with various materials need storage space (shelves for blocks, musical instruments, dramatic play, etc.), and
5. that dividers should be used to help contain the centers (these can be bookshelves, bulletin boards, room dividers, etc.).

A good classroom arrangement is one of the best ways to facilitate learning. Once children know where everything is, they can be taught the rules of each center and the proper use of materials. This knowledge will maximize free play and independent work.

Figure 1 shows a typical organization for a preschool or kindergarten classroom. The "circle" and "work" tables are areas for small-group work. The storage areas are used to keep the activity folders and blocks, art, and science supplies. The housekeeping area (play furniture) has storage boxes for dress-up and dramatic play materials. The large-group area is for all large-group activities, including music, movement, and storytelling. The work boxes are for independent work. The kitchen is for activities involving food and some science work.

This layout is ideal in that all traffic flow moves away from the large group. Once the children engage in a large-group activity, they can then scatter in various directions to small groups, free play, and independent work.

Materials

Almost all materials required by these activities can be found in the typical preschool or kindergarten.

SAMPLE OF MATERIALS		
aprons	flashlight	paper, plain
bags, plastic	foil	paste
bags, shopping	food coloring	paste sticks
balls	fruit	picture cards
balloons	funnels	playdough
beads	gloves	projector, over-head
beanbags	hats	projector, slide
beans	hole-punchers	puppets
bells	jars	puzzles
blocks	jewelry	record player
bowls	kitchenware	rings
brushes	macaroni	ring binder
cans	magazines	rolling pin
cards	magic markers	rope
cardboard	mat	rug
card stock	math sticks	sandpaper
chalk	milk cartons	scissors
clothes	mirrors	shapes
clothespins	musical instru-ments	shoes
color cards	newspapers	shoeboxes
cookie cutters	note cards	sticks
craft sticks	oaktag	smocks
cups	paper, butcher	songs
dolls	paper, construc-tion	sponges
dowels	paper, mural	storybooks
fingerpaints		tape
flannelboard		toys
flannel characters		

It is entirely permissible to substitute materials when what you have on hand will achieve the same ends as the materials specified. For example, when you do not have a particular picture card—either from a kit (e.g., Peabody, DLM, SRA) or other source—simply clip an appropriate picture from a magazine, mail-order catalog, or workbook, put it on a card, and use it instead.

Try to have materials for each activity organized well in advance of its scheduled use. Design and package materials so they will last from year to year—laminate when possible and use heavy gauge posterboard for cards and pictures.

The best way to store materials for each activity is in a file folder or box with the activity's name written in black marker ink. Keep the folders and boxes in the interest centers with matching labels on the shelves for consistent storage and easy access.

Parents

Preschoolers and kindergarteners learn best when parents are involved in the learning process. To help involve parents:

1. **Use displays.** Put art-and-craft activities of the youngsters on display, label them with the children's names, and invite parents in to take a look at every opportunity.
2. **Send notes and newsletters home.** Use notes and newsletters to let parents know what their youngsters are working on in school each week.
3. **Offer invitations.** Ask parents to come to school to observe the class at work or to serve as classroom aides. Through these experiences, they will gain an idea of how to work with the child at home.

Young parents, especially, often feel that their children should be moving ahead more rapidly than they are. Occasionally, a parent of a four-year-old will explain to the teacher how exasperated he or she has become after trying to teach the child to read. The teacher is the best professional to explain that complex tasks such as reading are very advanced and depend on the acquisition of many lower-level skills—skills such as those found under the visual, listening, and language categories of this book. Once parents understand more about early learning, they also understand how to give their children the best possible start in school, and at home.

Origins

The learning activities in this book are selected and adapted from the *Carolina Developmental Curriculum (CDC),* of the Frank Porter Graham Child Development Center of the University of North Carolina at Chapel Hill. The CDC had its start in a program developed in the Wake County Public School System (Raleigh, NC), the federally funded Project First Chance—Mainstream. Project First Chance was begun in 1976 for children aged three to six with mild-to-moderate delays in development. Its goal was to help children acquire the broad range of skills needed to function well in school.

Between 1976 and 1979, learning activities were developed and widely field-tested in preschool classrooms served by the project. The result of the work is a three-volume curriculum of carefully sequenced activities. Initially the CDC program consisted of two resource volumes: *Activities in Gross Motor, Fine Motor, and Visual Perception* and *Activities in Reasoning, Receptive Language, and Expressive Language,* together with the Carolina Developmental Profile, an assessment instrument to be used with the full curriculum, by David L. Lillie and Gloria Harbin of the Frank Porter Graham Child Development Center. The profile is a list of key criterion-referenced tasks—organized by age level—that normal two-, three-, four-, and five-year-olds should be able to do.

The original curriculum was organized around the six developmental areas of the profile—gross motor, fine motor, visual perception, reasoning, receptive language, and expressive language.

The developmental areas reflect the seminal work of two pioneers in the study of human development: L. L. Thurstone and Jean Piaget.

Thurstone used factor analysis to parcel out the distinct components of complex intellectual and adaptive abilities—resulting in the identification of the six developmental areas on the profile.

The influence of Piaget's theory of the sequential stages of intellectual development and his study of preoperational thought has influenced the content and organization of curriculum activities. The activities are designed to enhance the skills that are the foundation of intellectual and social endeavor. Consequently, the emphasis is on developing a broad range of abilities, and not on the rote learning of isolated "practical" skills such as tying shoe laces.

In 1982, Dr. Lillie and two coauthors published the *Activities in Social Emotional Development* as the third volume of the curriculum. Dr. Lillie reasoned that the human values of sharing, cooperating, and caring for others are more important than ever in today's complex and busy society.

The early years of a person's life have a lot to do with the development of these desirable characteristics. People are not born with an instinctive desire to help, to cooperate, or to share with others. They learn these things. They learn from experiences, particularly those experiences provided within the family during the first several years of life, and in the preschool or day-care setting.

While the CDC was developed for youngsters with learning problems, it has proven widely useful in classrooms of normally developing preschoolers and kindergarteners—classrooms in which the teacher wishes to monitor progress and learning closely. For more information on the CDC—the curriculum and the profile—write:

Walker Educational Book Company
720 Fifth Avenue
New York, NY 10019

PART I

Large Motor Activities

Small Motor Activities

Visual Activities

ONE FOOT BALANCING

Purpose: To balance on one foot with support for at least ten seconds. (No special materials needed.)

What To Do:

1. Have the children stand against a wall facing you.

2. Explain: "We're going to play a game called One Foot Balancing. Watch me."

3. Demonstrate: "First, you have to stand up tall, with your arms out like an airplane. Next, you lift one foot. I say, 'One, two, three, four,' and you win! Let's give it a try. I'll help you at first."

4. Hold the child's arms out for balance. Have him/her raise one leg up at the knee and place the bottom of the foot against the wall. Count aloud, "One, two, three, four." Then switch to the other leg. Repeat two or three times for each leg. (The only part of the child's body that should touch the wall is the bottom of the foot.)

5. Gradually increase the length of time that the children stand on one foot. A possible rhyme while you play:
   "One, two, three, four,
   Only one foot on the floor.
   If you like, I'll count some more."

Follow-up:

Line the children up three feet from the wall. Explain that you are going to play a game called Candle. Demonstrate: "First stand up straight, arms stretched high overhead, and bring your palms together. Slowly raise one foot off the ground. Hold this position while I count to two." Count can be increased to five.

HEEL AND TOE

Purpose: To balance on toes with feet together and heels off the ground while coordinating with arm motion.

Materials: 2 records: one with a medium beat, one with a faster beat
2 sheets of construction paper, one red and one green

What To Do:

1. Have the children line up facing you.

2. Tell them that they are going to dance without moving their feet.

3. Play the slower record and demonstrate each movement separately:
   a. Swing your arms to the beat of the music.
   b. Bend at the knees to the beat of the music.
   c. Rock from your heels to a toe stand to the beat of the music.

4. Have the children do each movement separately with you. Then, repeat, synchronizing the three motions to the beat.

Follow-up:

Play a game called Traffic Light, in which the children must stand on their tiptoes while the red light is on. They can relax when the green light is on. Use sheets of red and green construction paper as the "traffic light." Vary the duration of the lights.

ACORNS AND OAK TREES

Purpose: To balance on toes for at least ten seconds; to learn the concept that many trees and plants grow from seeds; to understand that an acorn is really a seed.

Materials: An acorn
Pictures of an acorn, a young sapling, and a fully grown tree

What To Do:

1. Bring an acorn to class and let the children examine it. Explain that an acorn is really a seed, and that if it is planted in the ground, a large tree will grow from it. Talk about the fact that most trees and plants start out as tiny seeds.
2. Then tell the children that you would like them to pretend to grow like trees.
3. Display the three pictures in sequence.
4. Have the children imitate the three positions as illustrated, beginning with the seed (sitting) position.
5. In the last position, have them stand on their toes and move their arms like swaying branches for ten to fifteen seconds.

Follow-up:

1. Talk about how little children grow into big persons. Have the children show you how big they will be when they grow up. Again, have them stand on their toes for ten to fifteen seconds.
2. Play circus trainer, and have the children pretend to be circus animals. As one of their tricks, have them stand on their toes for ten to fifteen seconds.

CONTACT!

Purpose: To understand the motion of kicking; to learn the concept of aiming at a target; to kick a beachball with reasonable accuracy in a forward motion.

Materials: Large inflated beachball
Masking tape
Large (at least 2' x 2' square) paper target
Large empty carton such as a refrigerator or appliance box

What To Do:

Note: The important thing to remember here is that what the child is basically learning is *contact*—just being able to look at and kick an object. Distance and accuracy will come later.

1. Tape the target to the wall so that its bottom edge touches the floor.

2. With tape, make a straight line on the floor, about four feet from the target and parallel to it. Tape a second parallel line about ten feet from the target. (See illustration.)

3. Have the children stand on the first (inner) line and swing their legs to "warm up."

4. Then describe the activity as follows:
   "Now that our legs are warmed up and ready to go, let's see if we can kick this beachball at the target." Demonstrate by kicking the ball at the target.

CONTACT! (continued)

5. Give each child a chance to kick the ball at the target.

6. After everyone has had a turn, allow the more capable children to kick from the ten-foot line.

Follow-up:

1. Have the children play Kick 'n Catch with beachballs or other large, soft balls. Pair the children and have them stand about five feet from each other. Give each pair a ball. One child kicks the ball to his/her partner, who catches it and kicks it back. Gradually increase the distance between the partners.

2. Place a large box lengthwise on the floor and tape a line six feet from the edge. Have child place the ball on the line, take a step back, and kick it into the box. Demonstrate a good kick for them.

3. Play Kick and Chase. Each child kicks a ball the length of the playground by kicking it, chasing it, and kicking it again. Make sure a start and a finish line are clearly marked.

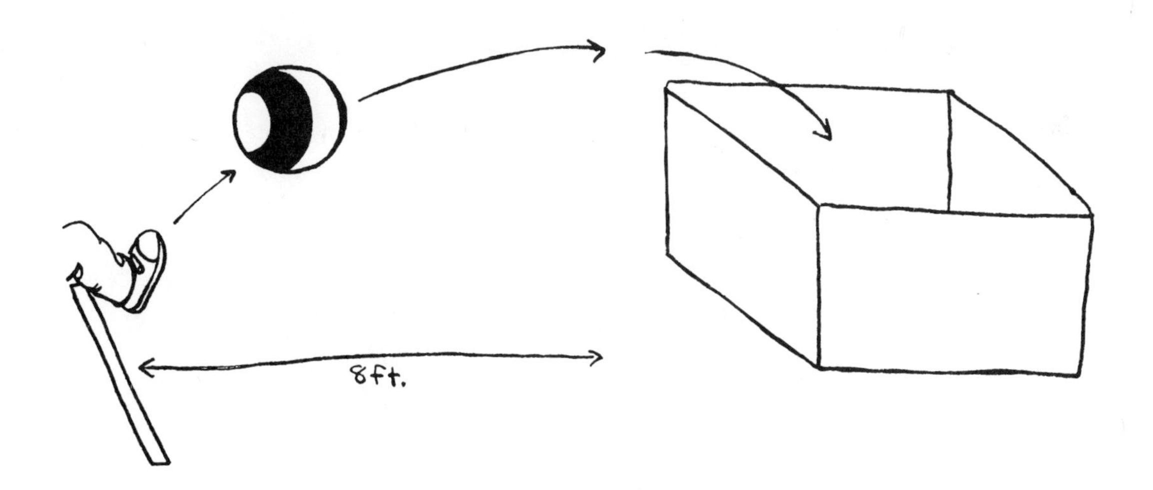

KNEE-HIGH JUMP

Purpose: To jump off the ground, raising one knee waist high, without loss of balance, and skip smoothly.

Materials: Large, sturdy balloon for each child

What To Do:

1. Tell the children that they are going to learn how to kick a balloon with their knees.
2. Demonstrate: Hold the balloon level to your waist with two hands. Then jump, raising one knee waist high, and kick the balloon from your hands. (See illustration.) Emphasize that both feet leave the ground.
3. Have the children practice the motion without the balloon.
4. Then give them each a balloon and have them kick away.
5. Encourage them to get both feet off the ground. Some children may need to be supported at the shoulders.

   Note: This move is a basic part of skipping.

6. Have the children alternate knees to kick the balloon. Don't let them use only their dominant leg.

Follow-up:

Have the children jump this way to a slow drum beat. Make sure they alternate knees.

"FOLLOW THE YELLOW BRICK ROAD"

Purpose: To skip smoothly; to follow a winding path.

Materials: Tape or chalk

What To Do:

1. Draw or tape a winding path on the floor. (See illustration.) Make a second path if space permits.
2. Describe the activity as follows:
   "Today we're going to practice skipping. But we cannot just skip anywhere we want. We have to follow the path on the floor and go where it goes."
3. Demonstrate by skipping along one of the paths.
4. Then space the children far enough apart to prevent collisions, and have them "follow the yellow brick road."

Follow-up:

1. Divide the children into two teams. Have each team skip along a different taped path. The team that reaches the end of its path first is the winner.
2. Have a "Skip Day," during which the children skip, rather than walk, to their various activities. Watch out for "fender-bender" accidents, though!

MARBLE FILL

Purpose: To increase manual dexterity; to understand the concept of *one* or *single*; to practice counting skills.

Materials: 1 egg carton for each child (12 compartments)
12 marbles for each child
Small box or other container for each child

What To Do:

1. Put twelve marbles in each small container and place a container about six inches in front of each child.

2. Place an egg carton directly in front of each child.

3. Demonstrate the activity to the children. Explain that they are to pick up one marble at a time and place it in one of the cups of the egg carton. When they are finished, every cup in the egg carton should have one marble in it.

Follow-up:

1. Repeat the activity but set a time limit. Use an egg timer and encourage the children to place all the marbles in the egg carton before the bell rings. Set the timer at thirty seconds the first time. Gradually decrease the time to the minimum time in which all the children in the group can perform the task.

2. Have the children do the same activity, putting two, then three, marbles in each section of the carton.

SQUARE TRACINGS

Purpose: To understand the concept and technique of tracing over a previously drawn pattern; to trace square shapes.

Materials:
Templates of different-size squares
Heavy white paper or white construction paper, 1 sheet per child
Thin white paper or tracing paper, 1 sheet per child
Thick black felt-tip pens
Crayons
Paper clips

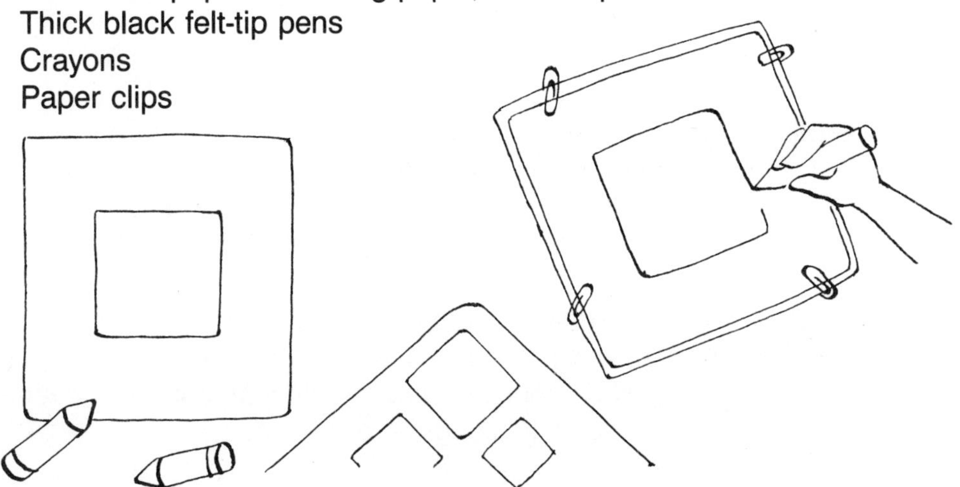

What To Do:

1. Using a template, draw two squares of different sizes on each sheet of heavy white paper. Use different-size combinations on each sheet.

2. With paper clips, attach a piece of tracing paper on top of each sheet of heavy paper.
   Give one set of papers to each child. Demonstrate how to trace over the lines that show through the thin paper.

3. Have the children trace their squares and fill in the shapes with different colors.

Follow-up:

1. Repeat the activity, using templates of different-size circles and triangles to create shapes for the children to trace and color.

2. Leave the templates and drawing materials in the art center to be used by the children during free play.

3. Choose the neatest tracings and display a colorful assortment of different-size squares on a bulletin board.

POPSICLE STICK FRAMES

Purpose: To understand what a square shape is and to recognize it on sight; to make a square out of popsicle sticks.

Materials: 1 piece of white paper for each child (approximately 5" square)
Popsicle sticks (4 per child)
Crayons or paints
Glue/paste and tape
Short pieces of yarn

What To Do:

1. Ask the children to draw a picture on their papers. Provide suggestions for picture subjects, if necessary.

2. Then tell the children that their pictures are pretty enough to frame. Show the children how to lay one stick across the top of the picture, then a second stick along the side (ends of sticks should just touch, not overlap), then across the bottom, and finally along the other side.

3. Have the children paste their frames to the paper. (Glue is needed only at the ends of each stick.)

4. Finally, have them glue or tape a loop of yarn to the back of the picture for a hanger.
   Hang the pictures on the wall or bulletin board.

POPSICLE STICK FRAMES (continued)

5. Explain to the children that all the frames they made were in the shape of a square. Show them that all four sides of a square are the same length. Point out, or make, rectangular shapes and explain how these have square corners but sides that are not the same length.

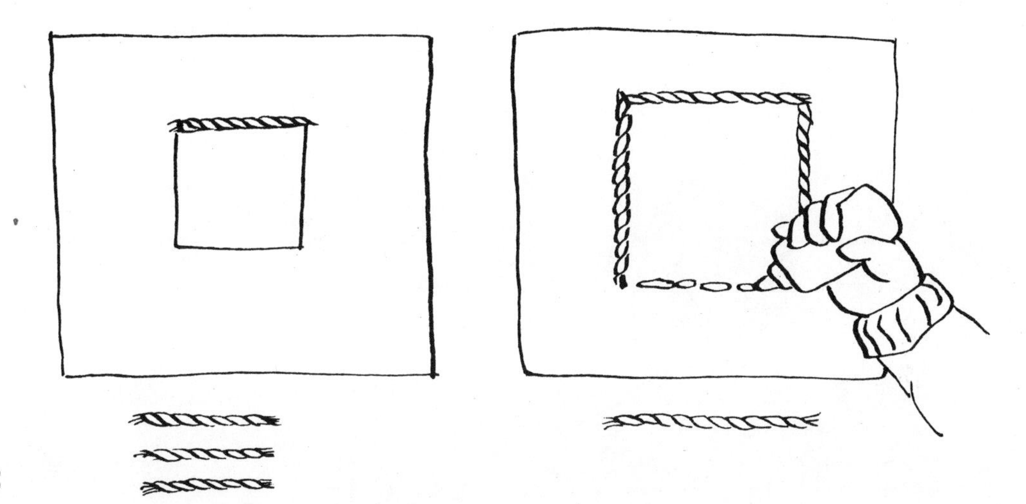

Follow-up:

1. Provide the children with strips of paper, yarn, or material that are color-coded according to length. Give each child a sheet of paper on which you have drawn a square. (Squares can vary in size from one page to another, but for each size there must be a sufficient supply of colored strips the same length as the sides of the square.) Have the children paste four strips of the same color over the sides of their square. Remind them that all sides of a square are the same length and that children must pick out colored strips that are the same length as the sides of his/her square.

2. Gather as many blank index cards as there are children in the class. On each card, draw one of the following shapes: circle, triangle, square, (add a diamond and a rectangle if your group seems ready for them). Distribute the cards to the children; ask all those who have squares on their cards to hold them up, then do the same for the other shapes. Collect the cards, shuffle them, and redistribute them. Repeat the activity so that all the children will have a chance to identify the shapes.

3. Individually or in pairs, let the children sort a stack of shape cards into appropriate piles.

A BOX WITHIN A BOX

Purpose: To learn to copy a square from a sample; using prepositions and positional terms.

Materials: 12 x 12-inch squares of paper
Tape
Crayons or magic markers (several per child)

What To Do:

1. Tape your paper onto blackboard as shown.

2. Instruct the children to listen and do what you do.

   Example: Start at a point near the upper left-hand corner of your square and draw a line down almost to the bottom of the square. Verbally cue the children ("Start way up at the top corner and come down—but don't hit the bottom! And don't pick up your crayons. Leave them right where you stop. Now draw a line *across* your square almost to the edge. Stop! Now back *up* almost to the top. *Stop!* Now back *across*—back to where you started. See, you made a new square.")

A BOX WITHIN A BOX (continued)

3. Then show them how to make a square within a square.

   Example: "Now take a different colored crayon and let's make a square inside the first one." Have the children start at a point two or three inches inside the first square.

4. Repeat the process using verbal cues *down, stop, across, up,* and *back over*.

5. Have them make increasingly smaller squares with different colors.

6. Let the children color the squares they have drawn.

Follow-up:

1. Have the children do the same activity on larger paper. Then cut out the squares with an *exacto* knife. Glue yarn down the center of the squares—you and the children have made a mobile.

2. Following the procedure that you used for demonstrating the nested squares, have the children draw concentric circles, ovals, and triangles. They can color each band differently to make bright posters for wall or bulletin board.

PAPER FLOWERS

Purpose: To develop manual dexterity; to learn the basic parts of a flower; to select and work wth different colors.

Materials: Lots of colored tissue paper ($4\frac{1}{2}$ x $4\frac{1}{2}$-inch pieces)
White craft glue/paste
Shallow tray
Large piece of posterboard

What To Do:

1. On the posterboard, make a large drawing of flower stems and leaves—omit flowers. (See illustration.) Explain the basic parts of a flower: stem, leaves, petals.

2. Tell the children that they have to help you finish the flower picture by making flowers to glue to the tops of the stems.

3. Demonstrate the ways to crumple the tissue paper to make "flowers":
   a. Squeeze it together with one hand.
   b. Roll the wad on the table or between your hands, using a circular motion.

PAPER FLOWERS (continued)

4. As children make their flowers, have them dip the flowers in a shallow tray filled with white craft glue.

5. Glue flowers to the ends of the stems. (See illustration.)

6. Assist the children in crumpling, rolling, and gluing the tissue wads to the picture.

Follow-up:

1. Using the materials and procedures discussed above, have the children fill in outlines of simple pictures with tissue wads.

2. Put a dab of glue on the end of a drinking straw and insert it into a wad of crumpled tissue. Have the children continue in this manner to make a bouquet of long-stemmed "flowers."

3. Using their created flower plants, or a plant in a container growing in the classroom, ask the children to point out the basic parts of a plant. You can discuss additional elements: roots, buds, flowers, petals, seeds, seedlings, etc.

STUFFED ANIMALS

Purpose: To stuff a paper toy with crumpled pieces of newspaper; to understand the differences between flat objects and three-dimensional ones; to create handmade toys.

Materials: Large sheets of paper such as that used for covering bulletin boards
Old newspapers
Patterns for simple animals or other objects
Paint
Stapler
Scissors

What To Do:

1. Cut bulletin-board paper into animal or object shapes (two of each). Shapes should be large and simple (e.g. whale, fish, turtle, pig, butterfly, fruit, truck).
2. Help the children staple the two pieces of each shape together around the edges, leaving a five- to six-inch space open.
3. Then have them tear pieces of newspaper, crumple them into small balls, and stuff them into the object through the opening.
4. Finish stapling the stuffed toys together.
5. Have the children paint them and add whatever features they wish, by drawing them and/or by gluing scraps of various materials to the toys.

STUFFED ANIMALS (continued)

6. Hang the toys up where everyone can see them.

Follow-up:

1. Have the children fill up white socks with crumpled newspaper to make sock puppets. Let them decorate the puppets with paper, yarn, etc.
2. Let the children stage a puppet show. Help them to make up a simple story that they can dramatize with their puppets, or adapt a fairy tale they all know.
3. Arrange the completed puppets on a shelf to make a cheerful room decoration.

CLAY SNOWPERSONS

Purpose: To understand the concepts of *circle* and *sphere* (ball); to roll clay into ball shapes, using a circular motion; to learn how to stack round objects in order of size.

Materials: Modeling clay or playdough

What To Do:

1. Tell the children that they are going to make snowpersons out of clay.

2. Demonstrate the two ways to roll clay balls:
   a. Roll the clay in a circular motion on the table, using one hand.
   b. Roll the clay between both hands in a circular motion.
   Point out to the children that in either method they are moving their hands in a circle.

3. Quickly make a three-ball snowperson for the children to use as a model. Point out that each ball is a different size, with the largest ball at the bottom and the smallest ball on top.

4. Give each child enough clay to roll one clay ball.

5. Have each child roll his/her clay into a ball, assisting where needed.

6. When each child has made a good ball, pass out slightly smaller quantities of clay for the second and third balls.

CLAY SNOWPERSONS (continued)

7. Show children how to stack the three clay balls to form a snowperson.

8. Give the children materials to embellish their creations with faces, arms, hands, hats.

Follow-up:

1. Leave the clay materials out for use during free play. Make some models for the children to copy, making sure that they are made mainly out of round balls (see illustration below).

2. Have the children name and discuss round objects found in the classroom, in the neighborhood, and at home.

TWO BY TWO

Purpose: To place and remove large pegs in a pegboard using both hands simultaneously; to develop hand/eye coordination.

Materials: Large pegboard and pegs for each child

What To Do:

1. Place a pegboard in front of each child.
2. Place about seven pegs on each side of the pegboards.
3. Describe the activity.

   Example: "Today we're going to play with these pegboards in a special way. We're going to move our hands together like this."
4. Demonstrate: Use both hands to simultaneously pick up and insert the pegs in the holes.
5. Then remove them in the same fashion.
6. Now it's the children's turn.
7. To make the activity more interesting, you might encourage them to pretend they are robots or machines such as cranes, steam shovels, etc.

Follow-up:

Do the same activity using smaller pegs and pegboards.

AN ACTIVITY OF SORTS

Purpose: To place a variety of objects in containers, using both hands simultaneously; to differentiate between sizes and shapes; to group like objects together.

Materials:
1 cupcake pan (or egg carton) for each child
2 each of small objects such as buttons, paper clips, poker chips, pegs, beads, macaroni, marbles, dried beans
Large shoe box to hold the items

What To Do:

1. Seat the children in pairs and place an egg carton directly in front of each child, and a shoe box between them.

2. Demonstrate the activity: Using both hands simultaneously, take two different objects from the shoe box and put each in a different compartment of the egg carton or cupcake tin. Continue until there is a different item in each of the egg carton sections. When the children have observed how you filled the pockets, empty the compartments back into the shoe box.

3. Tell the first child to follow your example and put the small items into the compartments so that each pocket contains only one type of item. Remind them that they must use both hands simultaneously, picking up a different object in each hand.

4. When the first child has filled all twelve compartments with a different item in each, the second child, again working with two hands at once, puts a matching object in each of the twelve pockets.

Follow-up:

Leave these materials out in the free-play area so that the children can practice on their own.

LETTERS HOME

Purpose: To fold a piece of paper to fit an envelope; to understand the concept of mailing letters.

Materials: 8 x 10" sheets of drawing paper, one for each child
Crayons and felt-tip pens
Business-size envelopes, one for each child

What To Do:

1. Give each child a piece of paper. Ask the children to draw and color a picture of something they did in school this week.

2. Have each child dictate a sentence about his/her picture, which you write on the "letter." Let each child print his/her name at the bottom of the sheet, and help those who need it.

3. Show the children how to fold the paper into three to fit into an envelope. At this point, exactness is not important.

4. Demonstrate how to close and seal the envelope.

5. Write the name of the child's parents on the outside of the envelope and send it home with the child.

Follow-up:

Paint a large shoe box red, white, and blue. Cut a slit in the cover large enough for the folded "letters" to fit through. Give each child a 1 x 1-inch square of colored paper and have the children glue "stamps" to their letters. Then show them how to deposit the letters in the "mail box." Explain that this is how real letters begin their journey. When the box is full, open it and distribute the "mail."

BUTTERFLIES

Purpose: To fold a paper square to make a triangle; to make a colorful "inkblot" painting.

Materials: White construction paper squares, 8x8" or 10x10" (one for each child); Scissors for each child; Plastic spoons; Paint; Paper punch; String

What To Do:

1. Draw a diagonal line down the center of each piece of paper and distribute the paper to the children.
2. Say: "We're going to make butterflies, and each one will be different. And we're going to use paint, but we're not going to use brushes! Watch what I do."
3. Demonstrate: Place a dab of paint along the line, then fold the paper in half along the line, forming a triangle. Press hard along the crease to distribute the paint. Unfold the paper and show the children the design you're made. Then cut out the design. Leave your "butterfly" on the table for the children to use as a model.
4. Have the children make their own butterflies, following the same steps. Assist each child as needed.
5. Attach string to the butterflies and hang them in the room.

Follow-up:

1. Attach the string of each butterfly to a stick or dowel and let the children "fly" their butterflies outside.
2. Have the children fold paper napkins on the diagonal and set the lunch or snack table.

PAPER BIRD MOBILES

Purpose: To fold a paper square to make a triangle; to make a mobile.

Materials:
Coat hangers
String
12-inch squares of construction paper, one per child
Scraps of construction paper or yarn
Pencils or wooden dowels, one per child
Scissors
Crayons
Stapler
Glue

What To Do:

1. Prior to the activity, prepare a mobile structure by suspending two hangers on different lengths of string from one coat hanger, and two more from each of these two, and so forth. Remember to vary the length of the strings.

2. Fold a square of paper into a triangle as the children watch. Insert a pencil or wooden dowel inside the fold; secure in place with a staple through the paper sides, just below the pencil.

3. Tell the children you are going to make a "triangle bird" by drawing features on the paper and adding a tail of yarn or paper scraps. Decorate the bird as illustrated.

4. Have the children fold, staple, and decorate their "triangle birds."

5. Remind the children to "make the ends meet" when they are folding the paper triangles, but do not assist them unless it is absolutely necessary.

PAPER BIRD MOBILES (continued)

6. Glue a piece of string to the top of each bird. (Use different lengths.)

7. Hang each bird from one of the coat hangers in the mobile structure. Two or three birds can be hung from each hanger. Display the finished mobile.

Follow-up:

1. Encourage the children to think of other objects that they could make from paper in order to create a mobile.

2. Have children fold large squares of paper into triangles and staple one of the open sides. (See illustration.) They have made paper hats! Ask them to think of other ways in which the cones could be used. (For example, to hold popcorn, as a funnel for sand.)

3. Hold a hat-decorating contest. Encourage the children to use their imaginations and decorate their hats however they like, using felt-tip pen, crayon, paint, construction paper scraps, and glue. Provide a theme, if you like. Have children model their hats and let the audience "judge" them.

STAND-UP ANIMALS

Purpose: To fold a square of paper to make a triangle; to create original characters out of folded paper.

Materials: 8" or 10" square of construction paper for each child; Scissors; Glue; Construction paper scraps; Yarn; Felt-tip pen or black crayon

What To Do:

1. Prior to the activity, draw a black square on each paper, as shown.

2. Give each child a paper square and tell them they are going to make "funny animals"; describe the method as follows:
   "This paper doesn't look like an animal, but that's what we're going to make—animals! Let me show you how to do it."

3. Demonstrate the steps as follows:
   a. Fold the paper into a triangle, with the square on the outside.
   b. Cut out the square. Explain that the points are the animal's legs.
   c. Quickly add a head and a tail, using construction paper scraps.

4. Using your animal as a model, assist the children in folding and cutting their papers.

5. Have them add heads, tails, eyes, etc. Encourage them to use their imaginations in adding different features.

Follow-up:

1. Let the children march their animals around the room in a "zoo parade."

2. Hang the animals on a "clothesline" in one corner of the room.

3. Leave the prepared materials in the art center to encourage children to make other designs by folding and cutting.

SAND TRACING

Purpose: To copy simple designs in the sand.

Materials: Sand table
Set of 10 large cards with simple geometric shapes drawn on them with magic markers
Set of 10 large cards with the same designs cut out of them

What To Do:

1. Dampen the sand slightly and smooth it out.
2. Tell the children that they are going to take turns "writing" in the sand.
3. Prop up one picture card so that the children can see it.
4. Have them copy the design in the sand.
5. Use the cutout cards with those children who are having trouble copying the design.

6. Place the cutout card flat on the sand. Have the child put one finger in the hole and trace the design. (You may have to help him/her get started in the right place.)
7. Remove the cutout card and place the picture card next to his/her tracing. Talk about how they are the "same."

Follow-up:

Make alphabet cutout cards. Have the children trace the letters in their names in the sand (one letter at a time).

PEGBOARD DESIGNS

Purpose: To create a design on a pegboard to match a sample; to observe details; to copy capital letters.

Materials: 10 by 10 pegboard for each child and yourself
Pegs of different colors

What To Do:

1. Make a row of pegs in a solid color on one of the edges of the pegboard.
2. Show your row to the children and tell them to make theirs like yours.

   Note: Turn your pegboard so that each child gets the same orientation.
3. If a child has trouble with spatial orientation (for example, makes his/her row down a side instead of across the top), have the child run his/her finger across both rows while you say, "See, mine goes across the top; yours goes down. Let's make yours just like mine."
4. If the child's row differs in color, point out the difference and help him/her start a row with the correct color.
5. Gradually make your designs more difficult, such as letters of the alphabet.

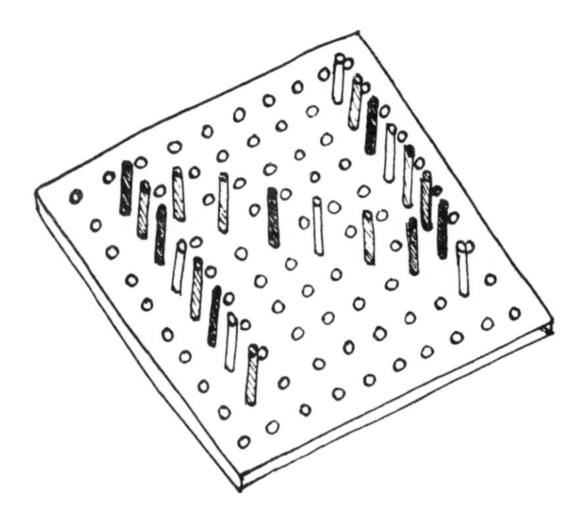

Follow-up:

Have the children create their own designs, incorporating simple geometric shapes and solid colors.

LETTER SHAPES

Purpose: To copy a design, using movable objects; to observe details; to practice positioning objects correctly; to copy capital letters.

Materials: Plastic straws
Popsicle sticks or coffee stirrers (cut a third of these to half-length)

What To Do:

1. Give each child four or five sticks.
2. Tell the children to watch what you do.
3. Place two sticks on the table to form simple letters: V, X, L, or T.
4. Tell the children, "Now, make a design just like mine."
5. When all the children have copied your letter, make another one, using three sticks instead of two (N, W, Z, H, etc.). Continue to build up to more difficult designs using four or five sticks, including half-sticks (E, K, C, S, etc.).

Follow-up:

Draw simple, straight-line letters on large cards, using a thick felt-tip pen. For example, form each child's name. Have the children glue straws or popsicle sticks on top of the lines. You will need to cut some of the straws or sticks into half-lengths.

DESIGNS SURPRISE

Purpose: To copy a sample design; to identify simple objects.

Materials: Drawing paper and crayons for each child
Easel or portable chalkboard

What To Do:

1. Seat the children around a table with their paper and crayons. Position the easel or chalkboard so that everyone has a good view.

2. Draw simple designs and shapes on the easel, one line at a time.

3. Have the children copy each design on their papers. Wait until they have finished each line before going on to the next.

4. Make the copying exercises into a game by adding an element of surprise.
Example: "Let's see what we can draw . . .
if we put a circle here
and a slanted line here.
Can anyone guess what it will be?
What if we put a line here?
How about that—an ice cream cone!"

5. Use directions like *down, across,* and *up* to assist the children. Point out shapes with which they are familiar: circle, square, triangle, etc.

Follow-up:

1. Make available a stack of 5 x 8-inch cards with designs drawn on them for the children to copy during free play or art period.

2. Encourage children to copy simple designs they find in magazines, books, etc.

COPYCAT GAME

Purpose: To copy a 4- to 5-piece block construction; to differentiate between objects of different shapes, sizes, and colors.

Materials: Sets of Tinker Toys, Lego blocks, or other construction toys that have distinctive pieces in several sizes, shapes, and colors (Ideally, there should be one set for each child)

What To Do:

1. Make a construction using *four* or *five* separate pieces.

2. Show your model to the children and challenge them to make ones *exactly* like yours. Describe your model. (Example: "The yellow bar goes right next to the red block.")

3. If some children have trouble, take your construction apart and let them imitate you as you reconstruct it, piece by piece.

4. Choose pairs of children to make constructions for the others to copy. Encourage them to use increasing numbers of blocks or pieces as they become more practiced.

Follow-up:

1. Have several sets of construction materials available in the play center so that pairs of children can copy them in their free time.

2. Encourage children singly or in pairs to make original constructions and be prepared to tell the others what their structures represent.

PUZZLE PUT-BACK

Purpose: To place a missing puzzle piece in the appropriate spot; to learn what a jigsaw puzzle is and how this type of "game" is played.

Materials: A 6- or 7-piece interlocking jigsaw puzzle (Each piece should be a distinct part of the whole picture. For example, in a car puzzle, one piece is the door, one piece is the roof, one piece is a tire)

What To Do:

1. Disassemble the puzzle while the children watch. Replace all but two or three pieces. Give the remaining piece to one child and ask him/her for some help. "I don't know where this piece goes. Can you help me?" Provide information that will help the child. (Example: "The tire is missing. Where does the tire go on a car?")

2. Disassemble the puzzle again and give another child a chance to complete it.

3. Gradually increase the difficulty of the task, asking children to work with puzzles of more pieces.

Follow-up:

1. Give each child pictures from old magazines, pasted on construction paper, as well as scissors and some glue or paste. Ask children to make their own puzzles by cutting their picture into three or four uneven pieces. Let the children try to assemble each other's puzzles.

2. Cut a large picture into four sections, each one having three or four uneven pieces. Give each section to a child to be reassembled. When all the parts are in place, have the children place their sections in the appropriate places so that the entire picture is complete again.

PICTURE PUZZLE

Purpose: To paste shapes onto a picture in the appropriate places; to recognize details in a picture.

Materials: A photocopy or mimeographed copy of a simple picture (such as those found in a child's coloring book); Scissors; Construction paper of several colors; Paste

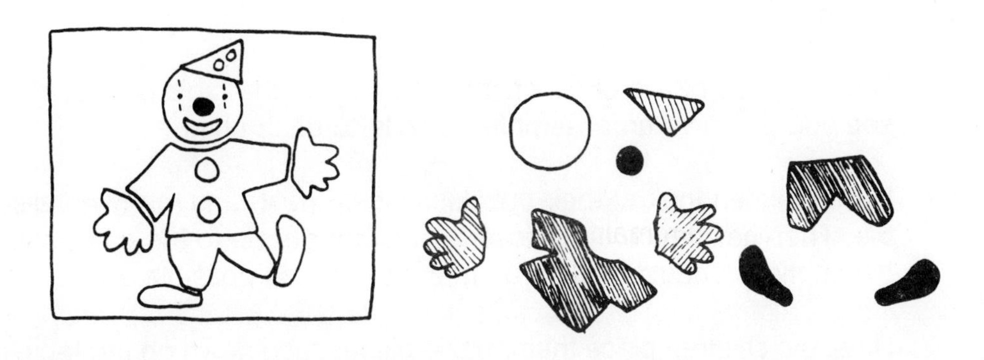

What To Do:

1. Make enough copies of the picture so that each child can have one, plus several extras.
2. Using an extra copy of the pictures as a pattern, cut the picture apart and lay the pieces out on a stack of construction paper sheets. (By using sharp scissors you can cut out five or six of each object at one time.) Keep the number of objects below eight. Talk about the shapes as you cut them out.
3. Give each child a copy of the original picture and one set of the cutout pictures that compose the picture.
4. Have children paste construction paper pieces into place to fill in the entire picture.

Follow-up:

Obtain two simple puzzles and mix up the parts. Give one part to each child. Display the pictures of the completed puzzles. Ask each child to decide which puzzle his/her part belongs to, and place it on the table in front of the correct picture. As children sort out the pieces in this way, help them to assemble them to make two completed puzzles.

PUZZLE QUIZ

Purpose: To identify a puzzle piece from a verbal description; to replace a missing puzzle piece in its proper position; to pay attention to details.

Materials: A different 6-8 piece interlocking puzzle for each child

What To Do:

1. Have a group of five or six children sit around the table so that all can easily see you and give an assembled puzzle to each child.
2. Have children look at their puzzles closely, noting as many details as possible. Then have each child describe his/her puzzle to the other children. The descriptions should include as many details as possible.
3. Have the children place their puzzle pieces face down on the table in front of them.
4. Take one piece from each child's puzzle. Place the pieces face down near you.
5. Pick up a puzzle piece. Don't let the children see it. Instead, describe it to them, for example, "I am looking at something that goes around a dog's neck."
6. The child from whose puzzle the piece was taken must identify it as his/hers. Return the piece to the child who identifies it correctly. Continue until each child has had at least one turn.
7. Allow children to complete their puzzles, turning over only one piece at a time.

Follow-up:

Have the children turn their puzzle pieces over and assemble the puzzles upside-down. (Child must cue on shapes because he/she cannot see the colors.)

STAIR STEPS

Purpose: To arrange a set of objects by size, from smallest to largest; to understand corect size sequence; to understand concepts of *short* and *long*.

Materials: Cardboard tubes cut to different lengths (tubes from bathroom tissue, paper towels, wrapping paper, etc.)
Blocks of different sizes
Boxes of same shape but different sizes
Straws cut into many different lengths

What To Do:

1. Stand three tubes on end. They should *not* be in size order.
2. Say, "Let's pretend we're building steps. The shortest tube will be the first step. Who can find the shortest tube?" Have the tube identified.
3. Then say, "Now look at the other two; which of these is the smallest?" Have a child select the right tube and stand it on end next to the shortest one.
4. Hold up the largest tube and ask the children where it should go to complete the stairs. Ask children to look closely at the completed arrangement.
5. Using different tubes with less difference in length, give a child three tubes and ask him/her to make "stairs."
6. Give each child a set of five or more tubes in graduated sizes and let children build their own sets of stairs.

Follow-up:

1. Repeat the above activity, using different-size blocks or boxes.
2. Ask children to arrange themselves in a line, according to their heights. The shortest child should be in front, the tallest in the back, etc.

COIN FAMILY PORTRAIT

Purpose: To arrange coins by size, from smallest to largest (irrespective of monetary value); to use coins as patterns to trace circles; to learn the names of different coins.

Materials: Pennies, nickels, dimes, quarters, half-dollars (or play coins), several of each; Sharpened pencils; Crayons; Strips of paper 5 x 9" (one per child)

What To Do:

1. Tell the children you are going to make a "family portrait" with the coins.

2. Explain that the family must be lined up in order of size, starting with Baby (the dime). You might wish to show children a real family portrait, or perhaps a drawing of a "family." This will help them to understand the concept of a portrait.

3. Put the dime on a strip of paper. Ask the children to help find Big Sister (the penny), then Big Brother (the nickel), Mother (the quarter), and Father (the half-dollar).

4. Demonstrate how to hold each coin in place while tracing around it, then demonstrate the drawing of features to make faces on the coins.

5. Help each child arrange a set of coins in the proper order; then let him/her draw a "family portrait."

Follow-up:

Collect several jar lids of varying sizes. Have a child place the lids inside each other, starting with the largest and ending with the smallest. Describe the assembled lids as a bull's eye. Then have the child draw a bull's-eye target by tracing the lids, one inside another, in the same order in which they were assembled.

FOOTPRINTS

Purpose: To arrange tracings of footprints from smallest to largest; to perceive size difference in similar objects.

Materials: Sheets of construction paper; Magic markers; Scissors; Crayons

What To Do:

1. Trace each child's footprints (with shoes on) on construction paper, and trace your own footprints as well.
2. Have the children cut out prints.
3. Take one of each child's prints. Write his/her name on the back.
4. Let the children compare the sizes of the different prints; then line them up in order of size.

   Note: If you have a large group of children, divide prints into groups of four or five that have obvious size differences.

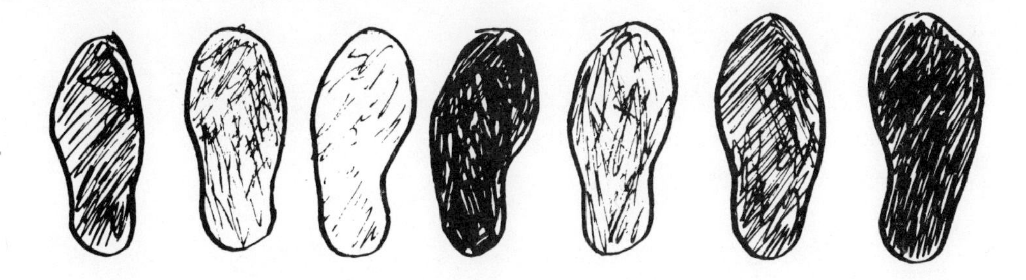

5. Prints can be thumbtacked to the bulletin board.

   Note: You may want to save one of each child's prints for several months; then repeat the tracing exercise so that children can compare prints and see how much they have grown.

Follow-up:

Measure each child's height. Cut lengths of colorful yarn to match the children's heights, and tape the yarn to the wall. Then have the children help you to rearrange the lengths of yarn so that they are sequenced from shortest to tallest.

PART II

Reasoning Activities

Listening Activities

Language Activities

YELLING AND WHISPERING

Purpose: To understand the difference between loud and soft sounds; to make loud and soft sounds on command; to understand when each type of sound is appropriate.

Materials: Tape recorder; Toy telephone

What To Do:

1. Tell the children to listen carefully as you whisper. Ask them if that sound was soft or loud. Then speak very loudly and repeat your question. Next, say a word like "kangaroo" twice, each at a different sound level, and ask which was softer.

2. Have the children, in sequence, call out their names. After each child says his/her name, ask the group if it was louder or softer than the previous name.

3. Make a tape recording of each child's voice as he/she makes loud and soft noises of various animals. Ask the group to judge which sounds are louder or softer.

4. Let each child talk in a normal voice, giving his/her full name and address. Play back the tape, asking, "Who speaks the loudest?" "Who speaks the softest?"

Follow-up:

1. Let two children, each with a toy telephone, carry on a telephone conversation. They should take turns talking "too loud," "too soft," then "just right."

2. Ask the children to help you make two lists. The first will be a list of places where it is okay to shout or talk loudly. The other will be a list of places where it is necessary to whisper or speak quietly.

STAMP FEET—LOUD AND SOFT

Purpose: To be able to identify loud and soft sounds; to produce loud and soft sounds by stamping the feet.

Materials: No additional materials needed

What To Do:

1. Tell the children that they can make loud and soft sounds with their feet as well as with their voices. Demonstrate by stamping one foot very loudly; ask children what type of sound you just made. Then stamp your foot softly and ask the same question.

2. Have children practice stamping their feet as a group. Tell them whether you want them to stamp loudly or softly, or at various sound levels in between ("a little louder," "a little softer").

3. Have each child stamp individually. Ask some to tap very softly at first, and gradually louder and louder. Ask others to start loud and work down to soft tapping.

4. Have the children march around the room in a line, stamping their feet loudly or softly as you direct them; ask them to stamp gradually louder or softer.

Follow-up:

When you take the children outside, have them listen very carefully for man-made sounds (trucks, cars, planes, playground noises) and natural sounds (birds, wind, dogs, insects). Make a list of all the sounds, loud and soft, that they identify. (You can build this "Sounds and Noises" list over many weeks.)

BICYCLE FUN

Purpose: To identify a bicycle; to be able to name at least some of the major parts; to understand how a bicycle moves.

Materials: A bicycle
Chart paper or chalkboard
Felt-tip marking pen

What To Do:

1. Bring a real bicycle to class. Discuss what a bicycle can be used for. Have a volunteer sit on the bicycle while you hold it and show the group how the bicycle moves.

2. Tell the children that a bicycle has many important parts. Then say, "We're going to play a game to see how many parts we can name. Look at my chart paper (or chalkboard). It says, Parts of a Bicycle. Every time someone can name a part, I will write it down on our list. Then we can count and see how many parts we were able to name."

3. Have the children take turns pointing to and naming each part of the bicycle.

4. Talk with the children about each bicycle part. Have them tell, to the best of their abilities, what each part does and how many of that part can be found on the bicycle (e.g. wheel, handlebars, brakes, seat, taillight, spokes, kick-stand, pedal). When a child points to a bicycle part such as the pedals, say, "Yes, the pedals are part of a bicycle. What do the pedals do? How many pedals does the bicycle have?"

BICYCLE FUN (continued)

5. When the children have named as many bicycle parts as they can, read the completed list to the children. Then say, "We made a long list of bicycle parts. Who can tell me one part of a bicycle? Good, the seat is part of the bicycle." Give each child a chance to mention a part, even if the same part is mentioned more than once.

Follow-up:

1. Make a simple jigsaw puzzle by pasting a large picture of a bicycle to a piece of oaktag and then cutting the picture into pieces. The piece should be cut so that each one contains a separate part of the bicycle. Let the children practice reassembling the puzzle by putting the bicycle parts in their correct places.

2. Using the chalkboard to sketch out highlights, tell the children: "Today we are going to 'write' our own story . . ." Start off the story with "Once upon a time, on a sunny summer day, the Jones family decide to take a family bicycle trip through the countryside . . ." Help the children make up the rest of the story from here. Draw appropriate pictures to accompany their story. Ask them questions such as "What kinds of animals might they see as they ride along?" "What kinds of buildings? . . . bridges?" "What buildings would they see in a small town as they ride through?" "Where would they stop for a picnic lunch?" "What adventures might they have?"

   Example: Child contributes, "One day he was riding along and the tire fell off." You draw a picture of a bike with a tire missing. "And he had to fix it with his tools." You draw a picture of a man using tools to repair a broken bike, etc.

THREE, TWO, ONE WHEELERS

Purpose: To correctly identify pictures of a bicycle, tricycle, and unicycle; to correctly state the number of wheels on each (using a picture as a visual cue, if necessary); to differentiate between one, two, and three things.

Materials: Pictures of a bicycle, a tricycle, and a unicycle

What To Do:

1. Display the picture of the bicycle. Ask children to name it and tell you what some of the parts of the bicycle are. Then ask the children how many wheels a bicycle has (while still showing them the picture).

2. Say: "We have talked about the bicycle and its parts. Now I have two more pictures. Let's see if you know what they are." Show the picture of the tricycle. Have the children name the picture and its parts. Ask how many wheels the tricycle has. Repeat the same process with the unicycle. (You will probably have to tell the children the name of the unicycle and explain how difficult it is to learn to ride one. Ask if any children have ever seen a real unicycle. Point out that in many circuses, the clowns often ride unicycles.)

3. Tell the children you are going to make the game harder. You will ask them questions but will not show them the pictures. Ask one child, "How many wheels does a bicycle have?" If the child has trouble answering, show him/her the picture and have the child count the wheels. Try to give each child a chance to answer at least one question.

Follow-up:

Discuss hazards of riding bicycles/tricycles on sidewalks and streets, and advise on safety precautions.

WHEELS EVERYWHERE

Purpose: To identify wheels on objects other than vehicles; to be able to name some objects with wheels; to recognize pictures of everyday objects.

Materials: Pictures of objects that contain at least one wheel; for example, sewing machine, roller skates, grocery cart, hand drill or other tools, wheelbarrow, furniture with wheels on the legs, wheels in engines and motors, telephone dial, dials on appliances

What To Do:

1. Hold up a picture of an object. Remind the children, "We have been talking about many things which have wheels. Who can remember something we have talked about that has wheels?"

2. Then say, "Today we are going to look at some more things that have wheels—things that we do not *ride* on. Look at this picture (object). Does anyone know what this is? Who can find the part that is the wheel? Good. Who can tell us how the wheel works?"

3. Display the other pictures (objects). Have children identify the objects, their wheels, and tell the number of wheels on each. Then discuss the functions of the objects *and* of their wheels.

Follow-up:

Ask the children to look for wheels or pictures of wheels at home and bring in a list prepared by a parent. Have the children work together to make a mural, using a long sheet of butcher's paper. Let each child draw a picture of one of the objects he/she found at home, or one of the objects discussed in the main activity above. Title the mural, "Wheels Everywhere."

EVERYTHING HAS PARTS

Purpose: To identify parts of various familiar objects; to state how many of the identified parts an object has; to understand the concept that most of the things in our daily surroundings are made up of different parts.

Materials: Pictures of, or objects such as, toys, vehicles, appliances, furniture, the human body, buildings (from magazines, catalogs, newspapers)

What To Do:

Note: The purpose of this activity is to extend the concept of *part-whole* from the bicycle to other objects. The activity can be repeated many times, using both old and new objects and pictures.

1. Hold up a picture or an object. Have the children tell you what the object is and what it does (its function). Then ask the children to take turns naming the different parts as you point to them, and counting them if there are more than one of each part.

2. For example, hold up a picture of a stove and say, "What is this? That's right, it's a stove. The stove is made up of many parts. What is the name of this part? That's right, it's a burner. How many burners does this stove have?" Continue in this way, pointing to the knobs on the stove, the oven door, the door handle, and so forth.

EVERYTHING HAS PARTS (continued)

3. In pointing to the different parts of an object, either start at the top and go sequentially to the bottom, or start at the bottom and go sequentially to the top, or start at one side and go sequentially to the other side. This helps the child in learning to look at and analyze objects in a systematic way.

Follow-up:

1. Make puzzles of different objects by pasting pictures onto heavy paper. Try to cut out the important parts of the object so that the children must replace the parts in order to reassemble the puzzle. (See illustration A.)

2. Draw simple pictures of familiar objects with some of the parts missing. Have the children draw in the missing parts. (See illustration B.)

3. Let each child choose a toy from the play area. Give the children time to study their toys. Then call on volunteers to talk about the different parts that make up their toy, and how many of each part there are.

4. Discuss parts of the body, using dolls to demonstrate. Have children name the parts of the head (eyes, ears, nose, mouth, lips, chin), neck, shoulders, arm, elbow, wrist, knuckles, chest, waist, stomach, hips, leg, knee, ankle, foot, and toes and tell how many of each the body contains.

CAR COLLAGE

Purpose: To identify a car; to count the number of wheels correctly; to name some of the major parts; to learn how to make a collage; to find the similarities between an object and a picture of that object.

Materials: Large toy car
Large picture of a car
Construction paper
Scissors
Paste
Magazines, old workbooks, catalogs, etc.

What To Do:

1. Hold up the large toy car and ask, "What is this?"

2. When children have identified the car, ask questions such as, "What are cars for?" "Are all cars exactly alike?" "In what ways are cars different?" "What is the same about all cars?"

3. Point to the wheels on the toy car and say, "The wheels are important parts of the car. How many wheels does a car have? Let's count them together." Ask the children to count as you point to the wheels.

4. Then say, "Now, let's name some of the other important parts of the car." Have the children take turns coming up, holding the car, pointing to a part, and naming it. (Windows, windshield, wipers, steering wheel, dashboard, seats, hood, motor, trunk, tires, rack, doors, roof, bumpers, fenders.)

5. Next, hold up a picture of a car. Have the children count the wheels (point out that there have to be four wheels, even if they are not visible in the picture), and then name some of the other parts of the car. Help them to recognize that the features they identified on the toy car can also be seen in the picture of a car.

CAR COLLAGE (continued)

6. Now give each child paper, paste, scissors, and old magazines and catalogs. Tell them to cut out all the pictures of cars that they can find. When children have assembled their pictures, show them how to paste them to the paper to form a collage.

7. While the children are making their collages, go to each child and ask him/her to count the wheels on one of his/her cars. If the child cannot count the number of wheels, use the toy car to review the subject with him/her individually.

Follow-up:

1. Take the children outside to the school parking lot to look at the different cars. Have them count the wheels of the cars and ask them how many each car has. Have them name other parts of the cars and talk about how some of the cars look the same while others look different. Discuss the most obvious differences, such as color, size, body shape, etc.

2. Give each child some clay, flour dough, or Play-Doh. Ask them to try to make a car out of their clay. Have children vote for the best-looking car.

3. Ask volunteers to tell the class about an experience they had during a ride in a car—on a long trip to a special place. Encourage as many children as possible to practice their oral skills in this way.

A WORLD OF CARS AND TRUCKS

Purpose: To identify a variety of vehicles and their various functions and purposes; to correctly count the number of wheels on each.

Materials: Pictures—wagon, tricycle, bicycle, motorcycle, car, van, small truck (pickup, panel), tractor, large trucks (moving vans, oil/milk trucks, dump trucks, car-carrying trucks, lumber trucks), tractor-trailer, bulldozer (and other earth-moving equipment), railroad car, airplane

What To Do:

1. Hold up the picture of the car. Ask the children what it is. Then put the picture behind your back and ask the children, "Who knows how many wheels a car has?" Encourage the children to answer as a group.

2. Then say, "Cars are not the only things that have wheels. Everything we ride in or that carries things has wheels that help them to move. Let's look at some of these other things."

3. Hold up a picture of a motorcycle. Ask, "What is this? That's right, it's a motorcycle. Who can find the wheels on the motorcycle? How many wheels do you see? Have you ever seen a real motorcycle?"

4. Repeat this procedure, using pictures of other vehicles.

   Note: If you use a picture of a train or a large truck, do not expect children to be able to count all the wheels. Point out that if there are three wheels visible on one side of a truck, there must be three more on the other side; ditto if four wheels are visible.

A WORLD OF CARS AND TRUCKS (continued)

5. When all the pictures have been discussed, line them up along the chalkboard ledge so that children can study and compare them. The purpose of this lesson is to help children realize that all different kinds of vehicles (things to ride on) have wheels, how many wheels there are on different types of vehicles, and what the wheels do.

Follow-up:

1. Have each child make a book entitled, "My Book of Vehicles." Each page should contain a picture of a different kind of vehicle. The children can cut out pictures from magazines and catalogs and paste them in their books on the appropriate pages. (A page can have more than one picture, so long as all pictures show the same type of vehicle.) Have the children name each vehicle; write the name on each page for them. Ask children to tell the number of wheels on each of the vehicles. Point out that larger vehicles often have more than four wheels.

2. Have children take their vehicle books home with them. Tell them to watch carefully whenever they are out walking or riding in a car. Each time they see a different type of vehicle, they are to put a check on the appropriate page in their books. After a week or two, have children bring their books to school. Count the check marks to find out who has seen the most different vehicles.

3. In free play or when reading aloud to two or three children, let them look at Richard Scarry's *Cars & Trucks & Things That Go*.

JUICE IN THE MIDDLE CUP

Purpose: To understand the concepts of *middle* and *end*; to identify an object in the middle position

Materials: 3 plastic or paper cups for each child and three cups for teacher
Fruit juice (enough for all the children)
Girl puppet or doll

What To Do:

1. Place three plastic cups on the table in front of you.

2. Fill the middle cup with juice.

3. Tell the children that you are going to tell them a story, and that the puppet will help you be acting out parts of the story. Let the children give the puppet a name.

4. Tell the following story:

   "Once there was a little girl named ______. One Saturday morning she helped her father clean out the garage. She worked very hard. Finally she said, 'Dad, I'm thirsty. May I have some juice?' Her dad said, 'Sure. There are three cups on the kitchen table. The *middle* cup has juice in it.' (Emphasize the word *middle*.) 'You may drink that juice.'

   "The little girl went into the house and saw three cups. She picked up a cup (pick up an empty cup) and carried it out to her dad. 'Dad, this cup doesn't have any juice in it.' Her dad laughed. 'That cup was on the *end*. (Emphasize *end*.) 'It wasn't in the middle. Go back and get the *middle* cup.'"

JUICE IN THE MIDDLE CUP (continued)

5. Place the empty cup on the end. Pick up the other empty cup.
   "She carried another cup out to her dad and said, 'Dad, this cup is empty, too.' Her dad laughed. 'That cup was on the other *end*.' (Emphasize *end*.) 'The middle cup is in between the empty cups. Go back and try again.'"

6. Place the empty cup on the end.
   "The little girl thought. 'The *middle* cup is in between the empty cups. Here it is!' (Pick up the middle cup.) 'Dad,' she yelled. 'I found the middle cup! Would you like to share the juice with me?'"
   Pick up the middle cup and show the children that it has juice in it.

7. Now give each child three cups. Fill the middle cup with juice. Have them identify the middle cup and the end cups. Encourage them to say, "The middle cup is the one in between the end cups." Then let them drink the juice as a snack.

Follow-up:

1. Move your cups around so that the cup with juice in it is on the end. Have the children identify the middle and end cups.

2. Fill two cups with grape juice and one cup with orange juice. Move them around and ask the children questions about the color of the juice in the middle cup.

3. Place two empty cups on the table. Give one child a cup with juice in it. Ask the child to place this cup in the *middle*, between the two empty cups. Let each child have a chance to do this.

WHO IS IN THE MIDDLE?

Purpose: To identify the middle object in a row of five objects.

Materials: No special materials needed

What To Do:

1. Have five children stand in a line and tell you which one is in the middle. Then have the children "scramble" the line and identify the middle child again. Repeat until each child has had a chance to be "in the middle."
2. Try this same activity with seven or nine children.

Follow-up:

1. Line up five blocks, all the same color; have the children point to the one in the middle.
2. Obtain pictures, stuffed animals, or puppets of five different Sesame Street characters. Arrange them in a line. Have the children point to the one in the middle. (If the children know the name, they may use it, but it is not necessary to identify all the characters by name.) Change the positions of the puppets and have the children take turns pointing to the one in the middle.
3. Repeat, using seven or nine objects in a line.
4. Challenge the group by asking them if they can find the middle of a row of six objects. Point out that the middle lies *between* the third and fourth items. To identify the middle object, point out that one has to pick two items, the third and the fourth, so that there is an equal number of objects at each end of the line.

COOKIE MONSTER'S COOKIE

Purpose: To understand the concept of *first*; to identify the first in a row of objects; to place an object first in a line.

Materials: Cookie Monster (picture, puppet, stuffed animal, etc.)
1 large, round, 4- to 5-inch-diameter cookie, e.g. large sugar cookie(if real cookies are not appropriate, substitute jar lids)
4 small, round, 2-inch-diameter cookies, e.g. vanilla wafers
5 colored circles, one on which to set each cookie

What To Do:

1. Line the cookies up on the colored circles so that the large cookie is first. Ask the children, "Which cookie do you think the Cookie Monster would choose if he could have only one?" Most of the children will reply, "The biggest one." Point out that that cookie is not only the biggest; it is also the *first* in line.

2. Discuss the concept of *first*: a) before any others; b) at the beginning; c) number one; d) the leader. Demonstrate by pointing to examples such as the *first* chair in a row, the *first* book on a shelf, the *first* letter in the alphabet, and so forth.

3. Leave the four small cookies on their circles and take the large cookie away. Position the Cookie Monster above the empty circle and say, "The Cookie Monster wants to have his big cookie. Who can put the cookie on the *first* plate? Who can place the cookie *first* in the row?"

4. Take the colored circles away, and remove the large cookie again. Ask the children to point to the cookie that is now first in the row. Then ask the children to put the large cookie back so that it is first once more. Give several children a turn.

OSCAR'S GARBAGE CAN

Purpose: To understand the concept of *last*; to identify the last in a row of objects; to place an object last in a line; to understand that last place is determined by first place.

Materials: "Oscar" from Sesame Street (picture, puppet, stuffed animal, etc.); 1 large wastebasket; 4 large coffee cans; 4 small toy animals that will fit in the coffee cans

What To Do:

1. Line up four small "garbage cans" (coffee cans) and the large "garbage can" (wastebasket), placing the wastebasket last (on the right end, as seen by the children). Place a small animal in each coffee can. Then talk about how Oscar loves garbage, and ask if everyone knows where he lives. Answer: In a garbage can.

2. Discuss the concept or meaning of *last*: a) at the end; b) after all the others; c) with nothing behind it. Demonstrate by pointing to examples such as the *last* chair in a row, the *last* car of a train, the *last* page of a book.

3. Talk about the garbage cans. Ask the children which one is *last* in the line (the large one). Ask one of the children to put Oscar in the *last* garbage can. Give several children a turn at this.

4. Take Oscar and his garbage can away and then ask the children to replace them in the last position.

5. Be sure to identify where *first* is at the beginning, and then periodically throughout the lesson. Try to help the children understand that *last* is always dependent upon where *first* is.

Follow-up:

Repeat the main activity, but use a smaller "Oscar" and five containers that are exactly the same. Remember to tell the children which can is *first* in order to help them identify the *last* can.

FIRST, LAST, AND MIDDLE

Purpose: To identify first, last, and middle on request.

Materials: 5 Sesame Street characters: Big Bird, Oscar, Cookie Monster, Bert, Ernie (puppets, pictures, or stuffed toys)

What To Do:

1. Line up the characters in whatever order you wish. Have the children point to the first one, the last one, and the one in the middle. It is not necessary for the children to know the names of all the characters.

2. Change the positions of the characters and have the children take turns pointing to the one in the middle.

3. Line up four of the characters. Give the fifth character to one of the children and say, "Please put ______ first (or last) in line," or "Please put ______ in the middle." Let children take turns placing the characters according to your directions. Try to involve all the children in the activity.

Follow-up:

1. Make five "tunnels" for the children to crawl through (boxes with both the top and the bottom cut out). Place them in a line and ask each child to crawl through the box you designate (first, last, or middle). Reinforce the activity by asking each child which box he/she just crawled through.

2. Draw a row of five circles or other designs on the chalkboard. Ask one child at a time to come up and erase the first, middle, or last, according to your directions. Try this with seven or nine circles.

WHAT IS IT MADE OF?

Purpose: Naming composition of everyday objects; categorizing

Materials: Pictures of everyday objects (from language kits or magazines)—some made of a single material, some made of many materials

What To Do

1. This game can be played as a quiz show. Show each child a picture of an item that is made from one material. (See Illustrations 1 and 2.) Ask him/her what that object is made of. If a child answers correctly, he/she can hold onto the picture till the end of the quiz show.

2. After each child has had two or three turns with pictures of simple items, introduce the more difficult pictures of objects made of two or more materials. (See Illustrations 3 and 4.)

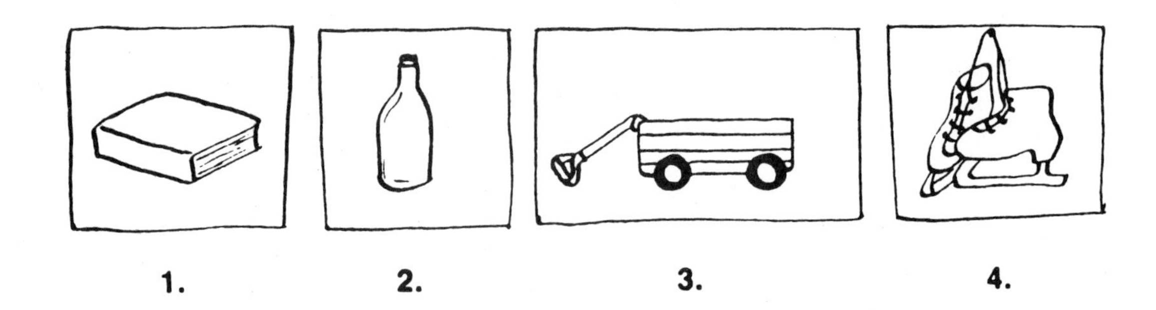

1. 2. 3. 4.

3. Say, "I want you to look closely at these pictures. These pictures show items that are made of many materials. I want you to name two . . ." (Example: A building is made of stone and glass.)

4. Show more pictures and ask the children to name three materials that the objects are made of. (Example: A car is made of metal, glass and rubber—also plastic and cloth.)

WHAT IS IT MADE OF? (continued)

Follow-up:

Set up three collection tables, marked as follows:

"Things That Are Made from Animals" (Examples: meat, milk and other types of food, wool clothing, a leather purse or wallet)

"Things That Come from Plants" (Examples: lettuce, apples, oranges, other types of food, cotton, cotton clothing, wood, rubber)

"Things That Are Made from Minerals" (Examples: brass fixtures, a small bronze statue, a small stone sculpture, nails, etc.)

Discuss with the children the three classes of objects: animal, plant, mineral. Provide them with simple information that they will be able to understand.

Example: "Minerals are found in the ground. Metal objects like nails and even car doors are made from minerals. Rocks are minerals too. The gravel in a driveway is a mineral."

Have each child bring an object from home. Have all of the children examine each object. Discuss its important characteristics with them. Then have them determine on which table each object should be placed.

If bringing objects from home is not feasible, have children bring in several pictures cut out from magazines that can be placed on the appropriate tables.

METAL—PLASTIC—WOOD

Purpose: To recognize the difference between metal, wood, and plastic; to identify objects made of these materials and sort them accordingly.

Materials: Several each of metal spoons and other metal objects, wooden spoons and other wooden objects, and plastic spoons and other plastic obiects

What To Do:

1. Hold up one of the spoons. Ask the children to tell what it is, describe its color, size, and shape, and tell what it is used for.
2. Then ask children if they know what the spoon is made of. If they do not know, tell them. Then introduce the other types of spoons and talk about what each type is made of. Use the words *wood, plastic,* and *metal* frequently as you show children the spoons. Try to help them recognize the differences between the three materials.
3. Have the children sort the spoons according to the material they are made of.
4. Then show them other objects, one at a time, that are made of wood, metal, and plastic; have them sort these objects and place each in the pile of spoons made from the same material.
5. Collect all of the sorted items, mix them up into a big pile, and have the children sort them again according to material (without your assistance).

Follow-up:

1. Ask the children to point to various objects in the room and tell whether they are made of wood, metal, or plastic.
2. Have the children make three separate "books"—a Metal Book, a Wood Book, and a Plastic Book (see illustration). Ask them to find pictures of objects made of wood, metal, or plastic, and paste them in the appropriate book.

WHAT IS A GLOVE MADE OF?

Purpose: To recognize and name different materials; to understand that the same type of objects can be made out of different materials.

Materials: An assortment of gloves made of different materials
Suggestions: Rubber gloves, transparent plastic gloves, wool gloves or mittens, leather gloves (baseball glove will do), oven mitt or cotton work gloves

What To Do:

1. Hold up one of the gloves. Ask children to tell what it is and some different things about it, such as what it's used for, how it's shaped, color (are all gloves the same color?), and size (are all gloves the same size?)

2. Then ask the children if they know what the glove is made of. If they do not know, tell them. Then introduce the other types of gloves, point out that they are made of different materials, and name the materials. Discuss some of the properties of each material with the children.

3. As each glove is displayed and discussed, ask children if they can think of any other objects made of the same material. You might be able to find examples in the clothing closet (e.g. rubber boots, a clear plastic umbrella, a wool scarf, a cotton jacket, a leather schoolbag).

Follow-up:

1. Talk about other items of clothing that can be made of different materials (hats are a good example). Ask each child to bring in an old hat from home; tell them the object is to collect hats made of many materials like the gloves described above. When the hat collection is complete, discuss the different materials from which they are made.

2. Obtain a copy of *Where Everyday Things Come From* (a Child Guidance Book). Read the parts on clothing, rubber, wool, and cotton. Read these stories one at a time, with plenty of time in between.

WHAT IS A HOUSE MADE OF?

Purpose: To understand the concept of *dwelling*; to understand that human dwellings can be made of many different materials; to identify the materials.

Materials: Pictures of human dwellings made of different materials: brick, stone, wood, glass, concrete, adobe, canvas (tents), skins (teepees), ice (igloos), grass (huts), bamboo

What To Do:

1. Show the children pictures of various types of dwellings. Talk about their appearance and what they are made of. Discuss why a certain material might be preferable to another and talk about the regions where certain types of dwellings are found. For example: "Here is a picture of a house that is made of ice. Does anyone know what an ice house is called? Where do you think people make houses out of ice? Why do you think they would do this?"

2. In addition to naming the material each dwelling is made of, discuss the properties of that material. For example, glass is transparent, breaks easily. Stone is very strong, cannot burn down, and will last for centuries. (Show them a picture of a castle.)

3. Ask each child to talk about his/her own home and the main materials it is made of. Have them draw a picture of their houses. (Accuracy is not important.)

Follow-up:

Collect pictures of different types of animal dwellings: ant/hills, bee/hive, wasp/nest, bear/cave, snake/hole, bird/nest, squirrel/nest, lion/den, etc. Have the children start a scrapbook of animals and birds in their natural habitats.

PICK A SHAPE

Purpose: To select the correct object, given a description of two of its characteristics (one in positive terms, one in negative terms).

Materials: Ten 8x10-inch pieces of oaktag or cardboard, divided into fourths with a shape in each section (Some shapes are black and some are light; some are obviously smaller or larger than the others)
A set of attribute blocks

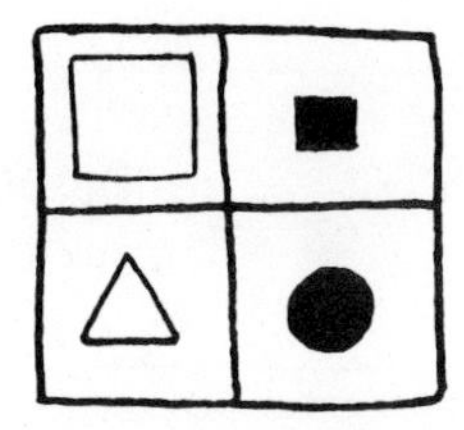

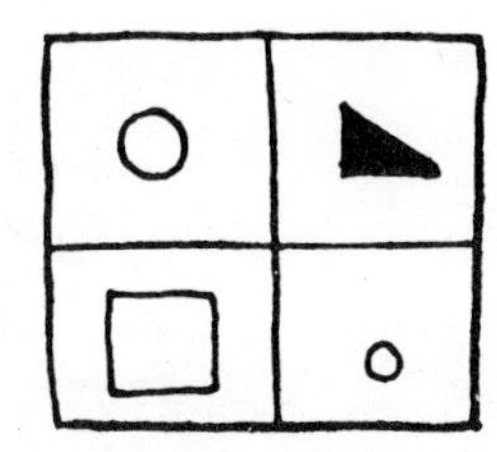

What To Do:

1. Hold up a card for the children to see.
2. Describe one of the shapes in both a positive *and* a negative way. (Example: Find the one that is dark but not large.)
3. Have a child point to the shape you've described.
4. Give each child several turns at identifying the shapes.
5. If the children are able, have them repeat the characteristics you've described. (Example: Child says, "This one is dark, but it's not big.")

   Note: Different clues can be used for each subject, so each card can be used for several turns.

Follow-up:

Using the same cards, have the children "help" you describe the pictures. (Example: Point to a big triangle. Say, "Look at this shape. It is big, but it is not a ______." Child replies, "But not a circle." Point to a small, dark circle and say, "Look at this circle. It is small, but not ______." Child replies, "But not light!")

FINDERS KEEPERS

Purpose: To differentiate between light and dark; to differentiate between round objects and cubes; to identify objects which share two characteristics; to follow directions.

Materials: Sets of the following objects:

Set A:	*Set B:*
Four white marbles	Four black marbles
Four black cubes	Four white cubes

Note: All these objects should be approximately the same size.

What To Do:

1. Place materials out of the children's view.
2. Tell the children that you are going to show them some objects. They must tell you "all about" each object.
3. Show them a white marble. Encourage them to talk about its color and shape. If they do not, hint at these characteristics yourself.
4. Next, show them a black cube. Again, encourage discussion of its shape and color.
5. Then ask one child to show you *"the one that is light and round."*
6. Ask another child to show you *"the one that is dark and square."*
7. Now show children the black marble from Set B. Compare it to the white marble. Emphasize that they are *"not the same."*
8. Point out the difference between the white and black marble.
9. Repeat Steps 7 and 8, using cubes instead of the marbles.
10. Finally, place all of the objects (Sets A and B) on the table.

FINDERS KEEPERS (continued)

11. Give each child a turn to find the object that you describe.

12. Remind them that they are looking for two characteristics. (Example: "Remember, you are looking for something that is black and round.")

Follow-up:

1. On a large table, put a sizable assortment of objects—tiles and blocks—that are different sizes (large, small), different colors (red, blue, yellow, white, black), and different shapes (circles, squares, rectangles, triangles); or blocks that are cubes, marbles, oblong blocks, or pyramid shapes. Ask small groups to work together to make different "collections" according to shape and size, shape and color, or size and color.

2. Hold a classroom "Size-shape-color Treasure Hunt." Give each child an instruction such as "Find something in the room that is small and white and round (or large and black and square, etc.)."

WHAT IT IS NOT

Purpose: To differentiate between large and small, light and dark, round and square; to understand that objects can have both similar and different characteristics; to recognize objects that share one characteristic, expressed in negative terms.

Materials: Sets of objects such as the following:

Set A (must be the same size)
Six circles
Six squares

Set B (must be the same color)
Six large blocks
Six small blocks

Set C (must be the same size)
Six dark blocks (red or black)
Six light blocks (white or yellow)

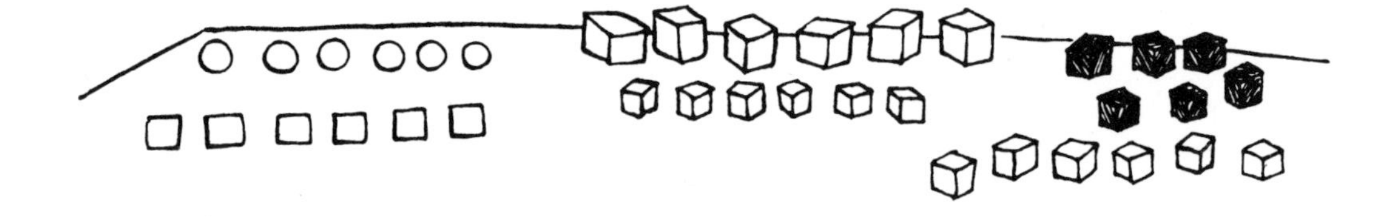

What To Do:

1. Have the children seated around a table. Place the materials by your chair, out of the children's view.

2. Tell the children that they are going to learn what some things are and what they are not. Say, "I will show you what I mean."

3. Place a square on the table and say, "This is a square. It is *not* a circle."

4. Remove the square and replace it with a circle. Say, "This is a circle. It is *not* a square."

5. Then place all of the squares and circles on the table and mix them together.

WHAT IT IS NOT (continued)

6. Select a child and say, "Find an object that is *not* a circle." Select another child and repeat the instruction, asking him/her to find an object that is *not* a square.

7. Give all of the children a turn at finding both a square and a circle, using similar instructions.

8. Repeat Steps 3 through 7 for the other sets of objects.

Follow-up:

1. You can expand the main activity by using different materials.

   Example: Squares, circles, or triangles of rough sandpaper
   Squares, circles, or triangles of smooth velvet

   Large covered jars of clear water
   Large covered jars of colored water

   Small jars of clear water
   Small jars of colored water

2. Play this kind of game with objects in the classroom. Describe an object, using both positive and negative terms, and ask the children to find the thing that you've described. Mention characteristics other than size, color, and shape. (Examples: "Look at this table. Find something on the table that is pointed but not short." Answer: a pencil. "Look on the shelf. Find something that is round but not thick." Answer: a record.)

MORE THAN ONE

Purpose: To understand the difference between singular and plural nouns; to demonstrate the use of regular plural nouns; to follow directions.

Materials: Several of the following objects: blocks, pencils, books, crayons, paper cups
Large box in which to place the objects

What To Do:

1. Seat the children around a table so that all can reach the box.
2. Take out one block. Show it to the children. Say, "When I have *one*, I have a *block*." Emphasize the singular *block*. Put it on the table.
3. Take out two blocks. Hold them up together. Say, "When I have *more than one*, I have *blocks*." Emphasize the plural *blocks*. Put them on the table near the one block.

4. Take out four blocks. Hold them up in both hands. Say, "When I have four, I have four *blocks*." Emphasize the plural *blocks*. Place these on the table, also.
5. Point to the one block and say, "*block*." Point to the two blocks and say, "*blocks*." Point to the pile of blocks and say, "*blocks*."
6. Now tell the children that you are going to ask them to get some objects from the box.
7. Then give each child a direction using a singular noun ("Please give me a cup"), and a direction using a plural noun ("Give me some cups"). Have them place the objects on the table in front of them.

MORE THAN ONE (continued)

8. Point out that when we want to talk about more than one of most things we simply add an *s* to the word. ("We say one cup and three cups. We say one bike and two bikes.") Ask each child to pick an object and talk about one of that object and several of the same objects.

Follow-up:

1. Give each child a sheet of drawing paper with a line drawn down the center. Tell the children that you want them to draw pictures of something they like. (Make sure that they choose something that has regular singular and plural forms.) On the left side of their paper they are to draw one item. On the right side they are to draw several of the same item. Call on children to describe the two pictures they have drawn. Examples: "I have a flower and three flowers . . . one lollipop and five lollipops . . . one face and four faces."

2. Collect pictures of familiar items (pencils, bikes, balloons, etc.) and make up two sets of picture cards. In the first set, paste a picture of only one item on each card. In the second set, paste a picture of two or more of the same item on each card. Make sure there is a singular and plural card for each item. Shuffle the cards and distribute them to the children. Then ask, "Who has the picture of a *pencil*? Please hold it up," and "Who has the picture of *pencils*? Please hold it up." Continue in this way until all the cards have been displayed.

ONE OR SEVERAL

Purpose: To understand the difference between singular and plural; to follow directions; to identify pictures that represent the singular or (irregular) plural forms of nouns.

Materials: The following pairs of pictures: mouse/mice, goose/geese, calf/calves, foot/feet, leaf/leaves, knife/knives, woman/women, man/men, child/children, elf/elves, wolf/wolves

What To Do:

1. Explain that most words can be changed from meaning a single object to several of the same objects by simply adding an *s* sound. But some words change quite a lot. Give examples of both regular and irregular plurals.

2. Give each child a set of cards (pictures). Review the names of the items on the cards with them.

3. Tell them that you will say the name of something and that they are to hold up the correct card when they hear the word.

4. Point to a child and say a sentence, very slowly, that uses both singular and (irregular) plural forms of a word. Example: "The mouse runs to play with the mice." The child with the mouse/mice cards holds up the *mouse* card, and then the *mice* card.
   Examples of other sentences:
   The black goose flies with the white geese.
   The calf romps with other calves.
   The leaf floats down to the leaves on the ground.
   The old man shows the young men how to build a house.
   The little child tried to catch up with the older children.

ONE OR SEVERAL (continued)

5. Collect the cards and redistribute them so that each child has one singular item and a *different* plural item. Tell the children that you are going to say some more sentences. Whenever a child hears the name of a picture that he/she has, the child is to hold up that picture. (In most cases, each sentence will involve two to four children. However, it is possible that the same child will have two of the words mentioned in the sentence.)

6. Make up sentences that use two or more different target words:
   The *mouse* was chased by some *geese*.
   The *calves* roll in the *leaves*.
   The *men* and the *women* cut the *weeds* with their *knives*.
   The *woman* raked the *leaves*.
   The *children* thought they saw an *elf*.

7. Have the children exchange cards and play the game again.

Follow-up:

1. Make up a story using regular and irregular plural nouns. Once you have established the main characters in the story (men, women, children, leaves, feet, rakes, baskets, trees, and so forth) pause before saying a key word and ask the children to call out the "missing" word. These words can be singular and plural, both regular and irregular.

2. Make ditto sheets of the objects listed in the above activities. Distribute one to each child; have the children circle the pictures of the plural forms of the objects.

LOTTO

Purpose: To understand the difference between singular and plural; to follow directions; to identify the picture that depicts a specified singular or (irregular) plural noun.

Materials: Dominoes or checkers to be used as markers
$8\frac{1}{2}$ x 11-inch paper, or card with 12 to 15 pictures on it—one copy for each child

Note: Some pictures will depict singular nouns. Some will depict irregular plural nouns. Some will depict "Fooler" pictures designed to distract the less observant child. (See illustration.)

What To Do:

1. Tell the children that they are going to play a looking-and-listening game. They are to listen as you describe a picture, look at their card to find that picture, and then put a marker on it. They must make sure that the picture they mark is *exactly* the same as the one you describe. (Demonstrate if necessary.)

2. Then give the following direction slowly and clearly: "Put a marker on the picture of ______." (Example: "Put a marker on the picture of the leaves.")

3. Continue until all the appropriate pictures have been marked by the children.

LOTTO (continued)

Follow-up:

1. Make a set of flash cards, each containing a picture of one of the singular or plural nouns that have been used in this group of activities. Hold up one card at a time and have a child identify the picture, using the correct singular or plural form of the word. (Example: Hold up a picture of three men. The child you designate says, "*Man*." You say, "Man is not the correct word. Would you like to try again?" The child studies the card more carefully and says, "*Men*." Say, "That's correct. The picture shows more than one, so the word *men* is right."

   Run through the cards slowly at first, then more rapidly as the children become more proficient at identifying the words correctly.

2. Line up all the flash cards on the chalkboard ledge; include a few regular singular and plural nouns (lollipops, flowers, faces). Place them in random order. Then ask, "Who would like to come up and take the picture of the lollipops (or faces, or flowers, etc.)?" Have a volunteer go to the board, find the correct card, and remove it. Continue until all the cards have been removed from the chalkboard ledge.

WHAT WILL HAPPEN NEXT?

Purpose: To understand cause and effect; to recognize logical sequence of events; to make predictions.

Materials: Ball (a large, lightweight type); Bowl of water; Cup

What To Do:

1. Begin a discussion that will encourage children to comment on what they think will happen next. Example: "If I pick up a pencil and put a piece of paper in front of me, what will I do next?" (Child: "Write something," or "Draw a picture.")

2. Encourage the children: "You're right. I am going to write something on this paper." Then say, "Sometimes it's very easy to tell what is going to happen next. What would happen if I threw this ball inside the room?" (Child: "It would probably hit something.") Say, "Well, let's see." Throw the ball so that it hits a chair.

3. Then ask, "What would happen if I put my hand in this bowl?" (Child: "Your hand would get wet.")

4. Provide another example. Pour a small amount of water into the cup and ask, "What would happen if the cup tipped over?" (Child: "The water would spill out.") Demonstrate, keeping a cloth nearby to prevent anyone from getting wet.

5. If necessary, devise several more "cause and effect" situations until the children have gained some understanding of the likely sequence of events resulting from an action. Remind them that it is sometimes very easy to guess what will happen next.

Follow-up:

Hold up a picture depicting some familiar action such as a bus pulling into a bus stop. Ask the children what they think will happen next. (Possible answers: "People will get off"; "People will get on.") Repeat with other pictures.

NOW WHAT?

Purpose: To understand cause and effect; to recognize logical sequence of events; to make predictions.

Materials: Plastic bag full of water; Large bowl; Pin

What To Do:

1. Hold up the bag of water and ask, "What will happen if I make a small hole in this bag?" Prick the bag with the pin (several times, if necessary) and show the children how the water leaks out of it.

2. Remind the children that "sometimes it is easy to tell what will happen next."

3. Then tell the children that they are going to play a game with you. You will describe "what is happening." They will act out what they think will happen next.

   Examples: Say, "It is time for our snack. What happens next?" The children act out eating their snacks.
   Say, "Play time is over and we are through with our toys for today. What happens next?" Children act out putting the toys away.

4. Continue with as many examples as are necessary.

Follow-up:

Play the game described above, using activities that have several steps. The children can role play their answers, or they can just talk about the events.

Example: Teacher: "It is almost suppertime. You are asked to go to the store to buy something to eat. What happens next?"
Child: "I buy some food." Teacher: "And what happens next?"
Child: "I take it home." Teacher: "And what happens next?"
Child: "Someone cooks it." Teacher: "And what happens next?" etc.

PICTURE THIS

Purpose: To interpret pictures correctly; to recognize logical sequence of events; to make predictions.

Materials: Sets of pictures (two in each set) from books or magazines depicting different actions

Examples: *Set A:* Children playing at the beach
Children building a snowman

Set B: Cat spotting a mouse
Man looking at a tiger in a cage

Set C: Child playing in mud in good clothes
Child sleeping in bed

What To Do:

1. Display the two pictures in a set. Encourage the children to talk about what they see.

2. Then ask a child to point to the picture that depicts the next action in a sequence.
   Examples:
   From Set A—"Point to the children who will get cold."
   From Set B—"Point to the one that will be chased by the other."
   From Set C—"Point to the child whose parents may get annoyed."

3. By describing different actions, you can use the same pictures several times.
   Examples:
   From Set A—"Show me the children who will get sunburned."
   "Show me the children who might go ice-skating."
   "Show me the children who might see fish."

PICTURE THIS (continued)

4. Let each child have several turns.

Follow-up:

1. One one half of a page, photocopy a picture that depicts an action. Have the children draw a picture of "what will happen" on the other half of the page. (See illustration for an example.)

   Distribute several pictures of this type. Examples of picture subjects include a) child sitting at top of slide, b) child pulling sled up a hill, c) child giving money to an ice-cream vendor.

2. Distribute blank drawing paper. Have each child draw a picture of what he/she does each night after dinner. Suggest that they draw several pictures in a sequence ending with going to sleep.

3. Tell or read aloud a familiar story, such as "The Three Bears." Stop at key points throughout the story and ask the children, "What happens next?" If children do not know the story well enough to answer, review the events that have already occurred in the story to provide clues.

PRETENDING

Purpose: To speak in full sentences.

Materials: Props for imaginary play
Suggestions: tools (hammers, pliers, screwdriver)
kitchen equipment
(pots, pans, big aprons)
bandage, doll
toy rake
toy broom
binoculars
steering wheel

What To Do:

1. Set the props out on a table or on the floor.

2. Tell the children that each of them is going to have a chance to "pretend" they are doing a grown-up task, using one of the props. The other children are going to try to guess what the "pretender" is doing.

3. Call the first child, ask him/her to select a prop and then pretend to do work with it.

4. Ask the others, "Billy, what do you think Jane is doing?"

5. Encourage answers in complete sentences. For example, "She is cooking supper."

PRETENDING (continued)

6. Then ask the pretender, "What are you pretending to do?" Child might respond, "I am cooking hamburger for my brother."

7. Encourage the children to expand their comments. For example, Teacher, while child pretends to hammer something, says,"Betty, what is Sam doing?" and child responds, "Working."
   Teacher: "Say, 'He is working.'"
   Child: "He is working."
   Teacher: "Is he fixing something? What is he fixing?"
   Child: "The stove."
   Teacher: "Say, 'He is fixing the stove.'"
   Child: "He is fixing the stove.'"
   Teacher: "Very good." (Turns to pretender.) "What are you doing, Sam?"
   Sam: "I'm fixing my car."

Follow-up:

1. During the course of the day, require the children to express their thoughts in lengthier phrases or full sentences. Do not accept one-word responses or comments from them.
   Example:
   Teacher: "Steven, will you please help me clean the chalkboard?"
   Child: "Yes."
   Teacher: "Can you say, 'Yes, I'll help you'?"
   Child: "Yes, I'll help you."
   Teacher: "I like to hear you talk in longer sentences. Do you think you can lift this box for me?"
   Child: "Yes."
   Teacher: "Tell me in a better way."
   Child: "Yes, I can lift it."
   Teacher: "Good! That's a better way."

2. Have the children put on a puppet show. Use a familiar children's story for a script. Each child operating a puppet must speak that character's lines using phrases and complete sentences.

SHORT SUBJECTS

Purpose: To interpret pictures correctly; to complete a short sentence begun by the teacher; to use complete phrases or sentences when speaking.

Materials: 8 to 10 action pictures

What To Do:

1. Tell the children that you are all going to look at some pictures together.

2. Tell them that you are going to say *who* is in the picture and that they are to say *what* that person is doing.

3. Select a child and begin. Hold up the first picture and identify the character. End your comment with the word *is*.

4. The child must then describe the action being performed.

   Example: Teacher holds up a picture of a little boy diving into a swimming pool.
   Teacher: "The boy is ______."
   Child: "Diving." (or "Swimming.")

5. Next, have the child repeat the whole sentence.

   Example: Teacher: "Very good. Now say, 'The boy is diving.'"
   Child: "The boy is diving."

6. If a child does not respond immediately after you identify the child in the picture, ask "What is the boy in the picture doing?"

SHORT SUBJECTS (continued)

7. Have the child repeat the whole sentence.

8. Give each child two or more turns at this activity.

Follow-up:

1. Have each child draw a picture of something that he/she likes to do. Then ask the children to describe their pictures to you. Print out some of the child's lengthier comments on the bottom of his/her picture and let the child put his/her name at the bottom. Hang the pictures around the room and read the children's comments back to them occasionally.

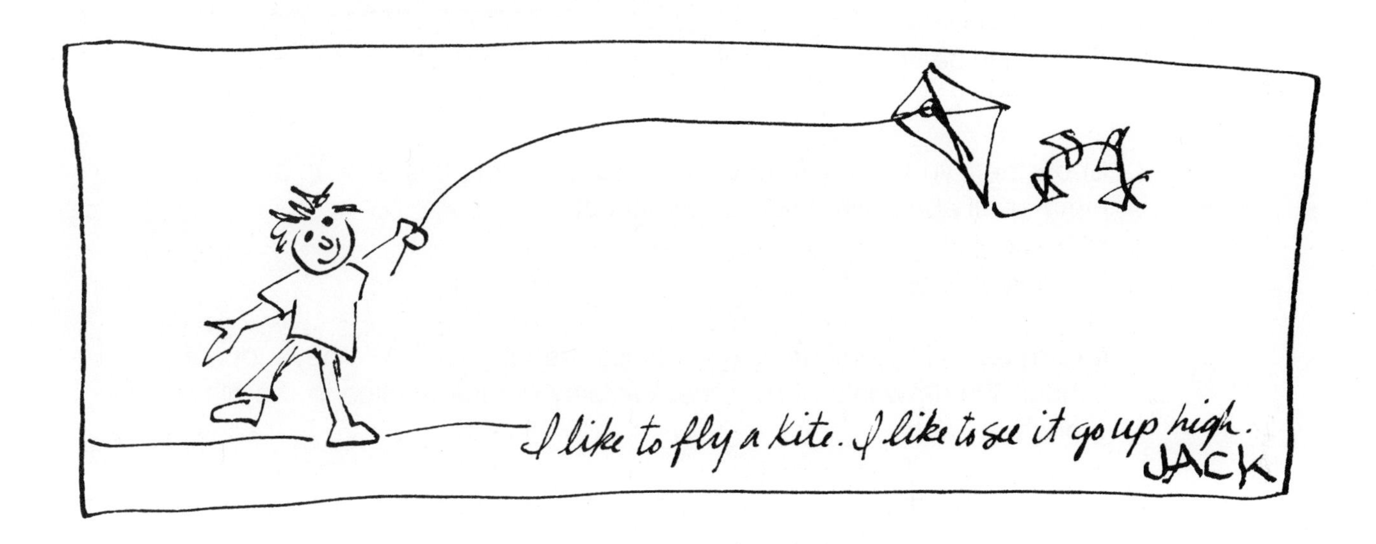

2. Take the children for a walk near the school. Point out various people in the neighborhood and ask the children to tell you what they are doing. Encourage them to speak in full sentences, as follows:
   Teacher: "Joy, do you see that man across the street?"
   Child: "Yes."
   Teacher: "I'd like you to say, 'Yes, I see him.'"
   Child: "Yes, I see him."
   Teacher: "Can you tell me what he is doing?"
   Child: "He is putting out the trash."
   Teacher: "That's right! And you said that very well."

A LETTER HOME

Purpose: To use sentences when speaking; to give reasonably complete and accurate descriptions; to dictate in complete sentences.

Materials: Postcard or 3 x 5 index card for each child

What To Do:

1. Pretend to be finishing a letter as the children are seating themselves for the next activity.

2. Show them your letter. Explain that you just wrote this letter to a friend, telling him/her all about what you do at school.

3. Read your letter to the children.

   Example: "All the children in my class are very nice. We have lots of fun at school. We draw lots of pictures. We play games outside in the play-ground . . .", etc.

4. Then ask the children if they would like to send a letter to their families, telling them about what they do at school.

5. Write down what each child dictates on a postcard, encouraging the child to expand on his/her comments.

   Example: Teacher: "Wendy, what do you want to tell your parents in this letter?"
   Child: "We play games."
   Teacher: "Don't you want to tell them that you play games at school?"
   Child: "We play games at school."
   Teacher (writing down child's comments): "And what kind of games do we play?"
   Child: "We play circle games," etc.
   Let the child print his name at the end of the letter.

A LETTER HOME (continued)

6. Mail the card home, or have the child take it home in an envelope. You may wish to send a note along, explaining the purpose of this activity and asking the parents to read the postcard back to their child and praise him/her for having "written" it so well.

Follow-up:

1. Ask the parents to do a similar activity with their child. The parents are to help the child dictate a letter to you, describing some of the things that he/she does at home. Read each letter that you receive to the entire class. Post them on a bulletin board and read them back to the children several times. Congratulate the children on how well they expressed themselves.

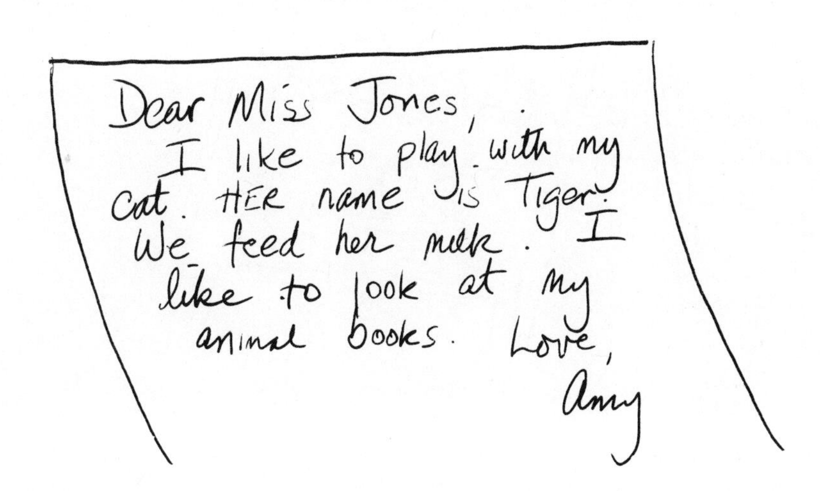

Dear Miss Jones,
I like to play with my cat. HER name is Tiger. We feed her milk. I like to look at my animal books. Love,
Amy

2. Tell the children that you are going to say the first part of a sentence. Explain that there are many different ways to finish the sentence. You will call on one child at a time to make up a different ending for the sentence. Remind the children that their endings must form complete sentences.

Suggestions: "When I opened the door . . ."
"It began to rain, so . . ."
"When Jack saw the parrot . . ."
"Mom opened the package and . . ."

AN ILLUSTRATED STORY

Purpose: To use phrases when speaking; to interpret pictures; to give verbal descriptions of pictures; to be able to extend a story line.

Materials: 8 to 10 large sheets of paper (12 x 18 inches)

or

1 very large sheet of paper (e.g. a 27 x 34 inch easel pad)
Tape recorder

What To Do:

1. Tell the children that you and they are going to "write a story" and that each of them will have an opportunity to make up a part of it.
2. Start the story off by a) drawing a picture of the central character doing something, and b) providing an introduction that "sets the stage" for what is to come.
3. Then ask one child at a time to fill in a part of the story.
4. Give each child one or two opportunities to contribute to the story. Children may also suggest drawings to illustrate the events in the story.

   Note: You may have to provide comments occasionally to keep the story "on the right track."

AN ILLUSTRATED STORY (continued)

Example:

Teacher (drawing a picture of a bear as he/she talks): "Once upon a time there was a bear named ______. Willis, what was the bear's name?"
Child: "His name was Sugar Bear."
Teacher: "Good! Once upon a time there was a bear named Sugar Bear. Sugar Bear loved to walk around and talk to other animals. One day he was walking along the path when he saw a ______. Natalie, what did he see?"
Child: "He saw a snake!"
Teacher (flips page and draws a picture of a snake; doesn't add facial features yet): "He saw a snake. Frannie, what was the snake doing?"
Child: "She was dancing."
Teacher (draws a happy face on the snake; adds wiggle lines): "She was dancing. Why was she dancing, David?"
Child: "Because"
Teacher: "You'll have to tell me something that I can draw. Why was she dancing, David?"
Child: "Because it was her birthday."
Teacher (adds a birthday cake to the picture): "It was her birthday!"
Etc.

5. When the story is complete, have the children retell it as you point to the appropriate pictures. Have each child repeat that part of the story which he/she contributed.

Follow-up:

1. During story time, have one child assist you in going through a familiar book and telling a story to the others. As the story progresses, require the child to fill in more of the story while you talk less.

2. Display a picture book that tells a familiar story. Show the children one page at a time, but do not read the text on the page. Instead, call on a different child to tell what is happening on each page of the story, using picture clues and recalling what has happened so far.

3. Over a period of several days, have each child dictate a story about his/her favorite holiday, or about a pet, or about a family trip or outing.

PART III
Social-Emotional Activities

HAPPY FACES

Purpose: To recognize emotions; to identify a happy facial expression on another person; to demonstrate a happy face; to understand that smiles and laughter are usually signs of happiness.

Materials: Pictures of people whose faces show different emotions
Large sheet of newsprint
Magazines
Scissors and paste
Small hand mirror (1)

What To Do:

1. Have the children sit in a circle.

2. Say, "I see someone who must be happy. I know this person is happy because I see a smile on his (her) face. Look around the circle and tell me who you see that's smiling."

3. Continue: "When we smile, it usually means we're happy. How else can we show happiness?" (Laugher, a happy and excited tone of voice.) "Let's all smile to show we're happy. Now let's laugh to show we're happy. Now, see if you can show me a not-happy face." (Pass around the hand mirror and let the children practice happy faces."

4. Now say, "I'm going to show you some pictures. When I show you a picture of someone who looks happy, clap your hands three times." Go through the pictures several times.

5. Next, tell the children you are going to teach them a song about being happy:
   "If you're happy and you know it, clap your hands.
   If you're happy and you know it, clap your hands.
   If you're happy and you know it,
   Then your face will surely show it.
   If you're happy and you know it, clap your hands."

6. Lead a discussion concerning those things that make us happy. Ask each child to name something that makes him or her happy and something that makes a parent happy.

HAPPY FACES (continued)

7. Then say, "Now we're going to make a collage. A collage is a lot of pictures pasted on a large sheet of paper. Let's each find a picture of someone who looks happy, and paste it on this paper." Give each child a magazine and scissors; help children paste the pictures they find onto the sheet of newsprint to complete the activity.

8. Finally, review the ways that people show happiness: smiling, laughing, shouting, cheering, clapping, jumping, etc.

Follow-up:

1. Ask each child to make a "happy face" for the rest of the class.

2. Read stories to the children. Choose books with many pictures of people and/or animals. Ask the children to identify those people or animals in the story who are happy. Pose questions such as:
   —Was ______ happy in this story?
   —How could you tell?
   —Why do you think he (she/it) was so happy?

HAPPY OR SAD?

Purpose: To recognize emotions in others; to identify and distinguish between happy and sad facial expressions; to demonstrate happy and sad expressions; to recognize the kinds of things that make him/her happy or sad.

Materials: Flannelboard
Happy and sad faces for the flannelboard (Appendix 1)
Mirror(s)

Note: You will need to make flannelboard faces, using patterns in Appendix 1.

1. Gather the children in a semicircle on the floor. All children should be able to see the flannelboard. Put happy and sad faces on the flannelboard.

2. Say, "We have talked about happiness. How can you tell when someone is happy?" (Smile; laugh; clap; happy, excited voice.) "Who will show me which of these faces belongs to someone who is happy?" Call on a volunteer: "Andy, place this star under the happy face."

3. Have a brief discussion and review of the things that make us happy. Sing "If You're Happy and You Know It."

4. Then say, "The opposite of happy is sad. When someone is sad, the corners of his mouth may turn down like this." Point to the sad face on the flannelboard. "Show me what you might look like when you're sad." Let children take turns making "sad faces." Let the children use a mirror to practice. Then ask, "What are some other ways we can tell is someone is sad?" (Crying; voice sounds sad; head is drooping.)

5. Continue: "It's all right to feel sad sometimes if something upsets us. What are some things that might make us sad?" Discuss, encouraging each child to contribute an idea. Discuss things that make grown-ups sad.

HAPPY OR SAD? (continued)

6. Tell the children that sometimes, when we feel sad, crying will make us feel better. Then ask what else we might do to feel better. (Play with a friend, look at a book, talk to your mother, etc.) Ask, "If we see a friend who's sad, what could we do to help him or her feel better?" (Put an arm around him or her; hold hands; ask child to play; help change whatever made him or her sad; e.g. find lost toy.)

7. "We have talked about being happy and sad. Tony, will you come and take the sad face off the flannelboard and give it to me. Let's all make a sad face. Now let's all make a happy face." (Praise children for their efforts and attention.)

8. Then tell children, "Today we're going to learn a song about being sad." (Sing to the tune of "If You're Happy and You Know It.")

   "If you're sad and you know it, wipe your eyes.
   If you're sad and you know it, wipe your eyes.
   If you're sad and you know it,
   Then your face will surely show it.
   If you're sad and you know it, wipe your eyes."

Follow-up:

1. Make up or read a story in which one or more of the characters are sad. The story could be about breaking a favorite toy, losing lunch money, a missing pet, etc. Then have children make a mural of sad faces. Take a long sheet of newsprint and have each child find a place along the paper. Distribute crayons; tell children to draw a circle and then fill in a sad face. Stress that the mouth turns down at the corners and the eyes are not big and wide. The child may draw in tears, wrinkles, etc.

2. Ask volunteers to tell a story about something that made them feel sad.

ANGRY FACES

Purpose: To recognize emotions in others; to recognize an angry facial expression; to recognize situations that could cause anger.

Materials: Flannelboard
Angry, sad, and happy faces for flannelboard (Appendix 1)
Crayons
Tape
Popsicle sticks

Note: Before the lesson you will need to make one happy, one sad, and one angry face for each child, using the patterns in Appendix 1.

What To Do:

1. Gather the children in a semicircle so that all can see the flannelboard.
2. Place the happy face on the board and ask, "How do you think this person feels? How can you tell?" Encourage the children to answer and talk about why the face looks happy.
3. Use the sad face to repeat the above activity.
4. Then say, "Today we're going to talk about another way we can feel. Sometimes, things happen that make us angry. When we're angry, we may look like this." (Place the angry face on the flannelboard.)
5. Ask, "What do you suppose made this person so angry?" Discuss some causes of anger, encouraging each child to contribute an idea.

ANGRY FACES (continued)

6. Continue: "Sometimes we become so angry that we feel like we just have to do something. We may throw something, yell at someone, hit something, or stamp our feet. When we try to get rid of our anger in these ways, we should be careful not to hurt anyone or anything. It's good to get our angry feelings out, and the best way to do this is to talk about how we feel and why we're angry. If something makes you angry in school, you could draw a picture of what made you angry and then talk about it. This will help more than yelling at other people."

7. Then tell the children you are going to teach them a new verse to the "feelings" song. It goes like this:

   If you're angry and you know it, tell us so—I'm mad!
   If you're angry and you know it, tell us so—I'm mad!
   If you're angry and you know it,
   Then your face will surely show it.
   If you're angry and you know it, tell us so—I'm mad!

8. Next, tell the children that they are going to make puppets with happy, sad, and angry faces. Allow children to color their pictures. Show them how to fasten the ice cream stick to the back of the picture to make puppets.

   Note: These puppets will be needed for the Activity How Did Bobby Feel? on page 96.

Follow-up:

1. Encourage each child to use his/her puppets to tell a story about how someone feels and why he/she feels that way.

2. Ask for three volunteers to role-play a situation in which one character is happy, one is sad, and one is angry. Let each child use the appropriate puppet to demonstrate how his/her character feels. If emotions change during the story, the children may change puppets.

3. Ask volunteers to tell about a time when they were angry, what made them feel that way, and what they did about it.

HOW DID BOBBY FEEL?

Purpose: To recognize emotions in others; to use puppets to demonstrate the emotion he/she would feel in a given situation.

Materials: 3 stick puppets for each child: one happy, one sad, one angry (See the activity Angry Faces, pp. 94-95, for directions for making puppets.)

What To Do:

1. Gather the children into a circle.

2. Tell the children, "Today we are going to use puppets to show how someone feels." Hold up the smiling face and say, "This is our happy-face puppet. How do we know that he is happy?" (He is smiling.) Ask children to give you examples of times when the happy face would be appropriate (e.g. when you get presents, during a silly game, when you play with a pet).

3. Repeat the above activity with the sad and the angry-face puppets.

4. Now tell the children you re going to read some stories. After each you will ask them, "How did Bobby feel?" The children are to hold up the puppet that they think shows the way Bobby felt, and then discuss and explain why they think he felt this way. Give each child a chance to share his/her opinion, as there may be more than one right answer.

5. Read the following stories:
   a. It was Bobby's birthday and his mother had baked him a big, beautiful chocolate cake. "Oh boy! Oh boy!" cried Bobby. "I love chocolate cake. It's my favorite. Thank you, Mom!"

HOW DID BOBBY FEEL? (continued)

b. One windy day Bobby was out flying his brand-new kite, when all of a sudden a big gust of wind pulled the string right out of his hands. As he looked into the sky, he saw his kite flying farther and farther away. "Oh no!" said Bobby. "I don't think I'll ever see my kite again. It's flying away!"

c. Bobby and his little brother Joey had just climbed into their beds when Joey ran over and grabbed Bobby's teddy bear. "It's mine now!" screamed Joey. "I want it!"

d. One day Bobby was late for school, so he began to run. As he came to the door he didn't see the big puddle of water there . . . Before he knew what had happened—SPLAT!—Bobby fell down and skinned his knees. His clothes were all wet. How do you think Bobby felt?

e. Bobby was looking at his new book. Jerry came over and said, "You think you're special because you have so many books. Give me that." Jerry grabbed the book and tore one of the pages.

f. Bobby was very excited. After school his mother was going to take him to the fair. When Bobby got home, his mother said, "I'm sorry Bobby, but I don't feel well. We can't go to the fair today."

6. This activity may be continued by making up more situations and different characters, each of whom feels happy, sad, or angry. Each time, encourage the children to talk about why the character felt the way he or she did.

Follow-up:

1. Decorate a section of the room with big pictures of people showing different emotions. Encourage children to identify how each person feels, and why. Children may enjoy making up stories about the pictures. These can be recorded on tape or written down as the child dictates.

2. Divide the class into three teams: The Happy Team, the Sad Team, and the Angry Team. Give each team the task of collecting pictures (from old magazines or workbooks) of people showing their team's emotion. Give each team a large sheet of poster board on which to paste their pictures as they collect them. Display the finished posters on a wall or bulletin board.

HOW WOULD YOU FEEL?

Purpose: To recognize emotions in others; to identify an appropriate emotion; to choose the mask which portrays an emotion.

Materials: 3 masks showing happy, sad, and angry faces (see Appendix 2)
7-8 magazine or newspaper pictures that will produce emotional reactions (e.g. spilled drink, circus clown, broken toy, delicious-looking cake, skinned knee)
Elastic thread or sticks to hold masks

Note: Before beginning the activity, make a copy of the three masks from the patterns in Appendix 2. Tie elastic thread to the masks so the children will be able to slip them on easily.

What To Do:

1. Gather the children into a group and say, "Today we are going to look at some pictures and then tell how they make us feel. We also have masks to wear so that we can make our faces show how we feel inside."

2. Show the first picture to the children. Ask one child to come up and pick the mask that shows how the picture makes her/him feel. Have the child wear the chosen mask as he/she tells the rest of the class why the picture makes him/her feel that way.

3. After the child has chosen an angry or sad mask and explained how he/she feels, ask the rest of the class, "How can we make ______ feel better?" Talk with the children about different ways to make a person feel better if he's sad or angry. When the child chooses the happy face, discuss with the children how they can share that happiness.

Follow-up:

1. Make a bulletin board entitled How Do You Feel? Divide it into three sections: happy, sad, and angry. Give each child a name card and let the children put their name in the area that shows how they feel at that time. They can move their name any time their mood changes during the day.

FINGER PAINTING

Purpose: To go to the bathroom and wash hands after finger painting; to understand necessity for having clean hands; to leave sink area reasonably clean.

Materials: Finger paint; Art paper; Newspaper; Paint shirt for each child

What To Do:

1. Seat children around the art table.

2. Say, "We're going to do some finger painting today. Who can tell me how we do that? What happens to our hands when we finger paint? How can we get the paint off our hands? That's right, we'll have to go to the bathroom (or sink, if one is available in the classroom) and wash the paint off."

3. Hold a brief discussion of wash-up and bathroom rules. For example: Be careful not to splash water on someone else; clean up sink area when finished; do not play or fool around in the bathroom; flush the toilet after using it; always wash hands after using the toilet.

4. Begin the finger-painting session and allow each child to complete a picture. As pictures are completed, allow children to use the bathroom to clean up. Remind them to raise their hands to let you know that they want to use the bathroom. Also remind them to clean paint from the sink area after they wash their hands.

5. Check bathroom periodically and praise children for following the rules.

Follow-up:

1. Review proper behavior for using bathroom. Place responsibility on child by trusting him/her to use the bathroom unassisted.

2. Ask children to think of different classroom activities after which they would need to go to the bathroom and wash their hands.

SNACK TIME

Purpose: To understand the necessity of having clean hands before eating; to use the bathroom unassisted; to overcome fear or shyness about going to the bathroom alone; to wash and dry hands unassisted.

Materials: Shy Sylvester stick puppet (Appendix 3)
Crackers or other snack item

Note: Before the activity you will need to make a Shy Sylvester stick puppet (see Appendix 3). This lesson may be presented before lunch instead of snack time, if you wish.

What To Do:

1. Gather the children around you in a circle.

2. Hold up the puppet and say, "This is Shy Sylvester the Cat. His real name is just Sylvester, but everyone calls him Shy Sylvester because he is afraid to do things alone. Let me tell you what happened to Sylvester one day." Tell the following story:

   "All the kittens in Sylvester's class were planting flower seeds. They were getting their hands very dirty. After each kitten planted his seeds, he would ask the teacher if he could go to the bathroom and wash his hands. Of course the teacher said yes, because snack time was next, and you should always have clean hands before you eat anything. Well, Sylvester was the last kitten to finish planting. When his teacher told him to go wash his hands, he said he was afraid to go alone. All the other kittens were eating their snacks, and no one wanted to leave to go with Sylvester. Poor Sylvester . . . he couldn't have a snack until he washed his hands. What do you think he should have done?"

SNACK TIME (continued)

3. Discuss solutions to the problem: 1) Wash hands by himself, or 2) Wait until someone was finished eating and could go with him. Ask: "Why would it be better for Sylvester to learn to go to the bathroom by himself?" (There isn't always someone available to go with him. Sometimes there is not room for more than one person at a time in a bathroom.)

4. Say to the class, "Now it's almost time for us to have a snack (or to have lunch). What do we need to do first? That's right, you need to go to the bathroom, then wash and dry your hands. Then when you come back, you can have your snack."

5. Allow the children to go into the bathroom in groups of a size appropriate to the facility. You may supervise the group, but allow them to use the toilet and wash and dry their hands unassisted. Have the snack ready when they return.

Follow-up:

1. When the children are engaged in a "messy" activity such as painting or playing with sand or clay, encourage them to raise their hands when they have finished and need to use the bathroom to wash and dry hands.

2. Ask the children to tell about things they do at home that make their hands dirty. Do they always remember to wash their hands before they eat? Have children tell whether they do this on their own, or whether their parents have to remind them.

RUFUS GETS A DRINK

Purpose: To behave properly while getting a drink; to know and observe safety rules; to display good manners. (No special materials necessary.)

What To Do:

1. Tell the children the following story:
   "I want a drink! I want a drink!" yelled Rufus as he ran out of the room. "Please wait, Rufus," called Mrs. James. "It's not time to get a drink, and besides . . ." CRASH! BANG!
   "Oh dear!" cried Mrs. James. "I think Rufus has fallen down. I'll bet he didn't see the two workmen out in the hall. I wish Rufus wouldn't run out of the room like that without asking."

2. Ask the children questions such as, "What happened to Rufus? Do you think Rufus was supposed to be running out into the hall without permission? Did Rufus show good manners? In what way was he careless? What is the right way to go get a drink?" Encourage all the children to participate in the discussion.

3. Next, review your classroom rules for getting a drink. (Children ask permission first, they push their chairs back under the table when they get up; they take turns; they wait in line without pushing; they do not put their mouths directly on the water fountain, etc.)

4. Say, "Now we are all going to get a drink. But remember, we are not going to be like Rufus!"

Follow-up:

Each time a child asks to get a drink, note whether he/she is observing all the rules that were discussed. If not, ask other children to comment on which rule was not observed, and what kind of accident could happen as a consequence. Praise children who follow all the rules.

QUINCY RUNS AN ERRAND

Purpose: To understand the responsibility involved when performing a task or errand independently.

Materials: Activity sheet, "Quincy Runs An Errand" (Appendix 4)
Crayons

What To Do:

1. Gather the children around you in a semicircle.

2. Say, "I'm going to tell you a story about a boy named Quincy McLean."

3. Tell the following story:

   "Quincy is a little boy about your age. He was always telling his mother that he could do things all by himself. Well, one day Quincy's mother needed some bread and milk from the neighborhood grocery store.

   "She said, "I need some bread and milk from the store, but I can't leave the baby now. What should I do?'

   "Quincy said, 'Mom, I can go to the store for you. I know the way.'

   "Quincy's mom said, 'Well, I don't know, Quincy. You've never been to the store by yourself before and I'm not sure you're big enough to go.'

   "'Come on, Mom, I'm a big boy now. Please, can I go?' Well, Quincy's mother decided to let him go.

   "She gave Quincy some money and said, 'I want you to get a loaf of bread and a quart of milk. Now don't stop and play on the way—go right to the store and come right back.'

   "Quincy said, 'I will, Mom—I'm a big boy, now. Bye.'"

(continued)

QUINCY RUNS AN ERRAND (continued)

4. Hold up the activity sheet (Appendix 4) or enlarge it on chalkboard so that the group can see it.

"Now here is the street that Quincy has to take to go to the store. But there are lots of interesting things on the way to the store that might take Quincy's mind off what he is supposed to do. And that's exactly what happened.

"Quincy left his house and walked along the street. And what do you suppose he came to first? A nice playground with climbing bars and swings and slides. (Using a crayon, or chalk, draw along the path to show Quincy's route.) Should Quincy stop and play, or should he go on to the store?" Talk briefly with the children about what Quincy should do; then continue the story.

"Well, Quincy stopped and played for a little while. First he swung on the swings and then he slid down the slide and climbed on the bars.

"'Oh, oh,' thought Quincy, 'I had better hurry. I forgot that I am supposed to go straight to the store.' So off Quincy went again toward the store.

"Pretty soon, he came to some children who were going for a walk. One of the girls called, 'Come on, Quincy, take a walk with us. We're going down this way.' (Use the activity page to show the road going off in an opposite direction from the store.) Quincy started to go with the children. But then he thought, 'Oh, no, I can't do that. I'm supposed to go right to the store.' And he told the children he couldn't go because he was running an errand for his mom. Was Quincy acting in a responsible way?" Talk briefly with the children about Quincy's choice, then continue the story.

"Well Quincy finally got to the store and bought the bread and milk. Then he started back toward home. Pretty soon he came to a large puddle next to the street. There was a boy sailing a little paper plate on the puddle.

"'Boy, that looks like fun,' said Quincy. He stopped to watch for a minute.

"'Do you want to play with me?' asked the little boy.

"'Well, maybe just for a minute,' said Quincy. And he put down his bag and walked into the puddle to sail the paper plate. Of course, he got his feet all wet. Quincy was having fun and then he remembered: 'Oh, oh, I'm supposed to go straight home.' So he said goodbye to the little boy, and off he went down the street.

"As Quincy was getting close to home he went by the playground again. One of the boys who was playing there called, 'Come and swing with me, Quincy.'

QUINCY RUNS AN ERRAND (continued)

"Quincy thought, 'I sure would like to do that.' But he said, 'No, I told my mom I would bring the bread and milk right home from the store.' And off Quincy went toward home.

"But before he got home he saw an airplane stuck in a small tree. 'Boy, I'd sure like to have that airplane,' thought Quincy. 'I think I'll just climb up in that tree and get it.'

"Do you think Quincy should stop and climb the tree to get the airplane? What would you do? (Give each child a chance to respond to the question.)

"Now guess what? Quincy put down the paper bag and climbed up in the tree and got the little airplane. But as he climbed down the tree, he saw that one of the wings was broken off. 'Oh, this plane is no good,' thought Quincy, and he picked up the bag and started home.

"When he got home, Quincy's mother said, 'Quincy, what took you so long? I was very worried about you.'

"'Well, I stopped and played for a little while, Mom,' said Quincy.

"Quincy's mom said, 'Well, I don't think I can send you to the store again until you get older, Quincy, because when I ask you to run an errand, that's what you have to do. You can't stop and do other things."

5. Talk about whether Quincy's mom should send him on another errand, and what Quincy should do if she does.

6. Discuss the wrong things that Quincy did, and also the things that showed he could do the right thing sometimes. Point out that one of the reasons why Quincy was wrong to stop and play was that he made his mother worry about him.

7. When you are finished with the discussion, hang the activity sheet on a wall or bulletin board.

Follow-up:

1. Provide opportunities for individual children to run errands independently (e.g. taking messages to the office or to other rooms in the building). As you send them off, remind them of the story of Quincy McLean.

2. Discuss the story of Jack and the Beanstalk. In what way did Jack behave irresponsibly? (Trading the cow for some beans.) Ask the children to think of other stories in which children did not show good judgment or responsible behavior.

WHICH ONE ARE YOU?

Purpose: To develop the habit of doing things for oneself; to act in a responsible manner; to recognize the value of taking part in helpful activities.

Materials: Several cartoons or comic strip pictures showing children engaged in helpful, responsible activities
Several pictures showing children doing a task irresponsibly or "goofing off"

Note: Many children will see different meanings in different pictures. Always allow them to explain their answers before you make any judgments.

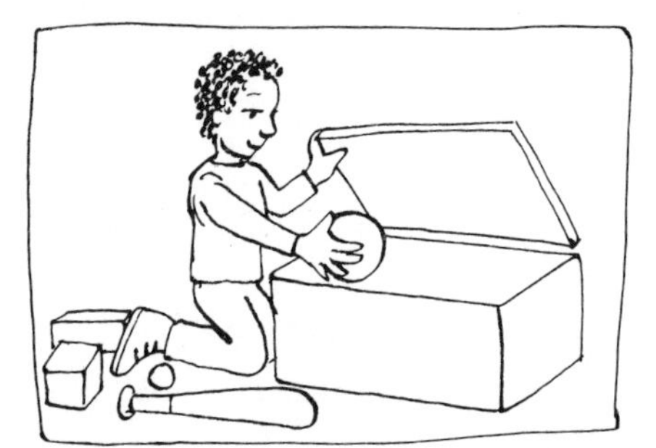

What To Do:

1. Show the children two pictures, one at a time. One picture should show a responsible child, and one should show a child acting irresponsibly. Ask questions such as, "What is happening in this picture? Which of the two persons would you send on an important errand?" Discuss the difference between doing the right thing and getting something done, and not getting the job done at all.

2. Encourage the children to discuss why it is important to do things for themselves and not wait for others to do it for them. Also discuss the importance of finishing a job once it has been started.

3. Continue this activity with several other pairs of pictures. For each pair, have the children identify the irresponsible child and the responsible one.

Follow-up:

At the start of free play, let each child tell you which area he/she would like to play in for the next 10 or 15 minutes. Allow them to be responsible for their choice and encourage them to follow through with their decision. (See Ypsilanti Study.)

OUR FAVORITE THINGS

Purpose: To respect the property rights of others; to understand the importance of asking to borrow something as opposed to simply taking it; to understand the importance of returning borrowed property.

Materials: Drawing paper; Crayons

What To Do:

1. Distribute paper and crayons and ask children to draw a picture of their favorite possession (toy, clothing, book, etc.).
2. When drawings are completed, allow each child to display his/her drawing and tell about his/her favorite thing.
3. After all the children have had an opportunity to share this information, ask each one: "How would you feel if someone took your ______ without asking you first? How would you feel if someone borrowed your ______ and didn't give it back?"
4. Discuss the point that each child has possessions that he/she does not want others to take without asking. Stress that *others* have property that we shouldn't take without asking. Ask children to name things at school that belong to other children (coats, hats, lunch boxes, projects) and those that belong to the teacher (books, papers, etc.).
5. End the lesson by asking children to tell what they learned about respecting the property of others.

Follow-up:

Ask each child to bring a toy from home. Before the play session, discuss the importance of sharing, of asking to borrow, of playing carefully to avoid damaging the toy, and of returning the toy to the owner when finished. Allow children to play with toys for 10-15 minutes. Encourage sharing toys with children who ask to borrow them in an appropriate manner.

LET'S MAKE A DEAL

Purpose: To respect the property rights of others; to ask to borrow a toy; to return the borrowed item to its owner.

Materials: An assortment of favorite toys, games, and other materials from the classroom (enough for each child to have something)
Timer or bell

What To Do:

1. Have a brief discussion reviewing the importance of respecting others' property rights: ask first before you borrow; be sure to return what was borrowed.

2. Tell children you are going to pretend that all the toys and other objects belong to you. They may play with any of them so long as they first ask you if they may borrow something, and then return the item to you and thank you for it when they are finished.

3. Have children take turns asking to borrow items. Set timer for 5 minutes. Tell children that when the timer rings they must return the borrowed items and then return to their places. If a child is finished with a toy before the time limit is up, he or she may return it and thank you for it and ask to borrow another.

4. When all the children are seated again, praise them for their efforts and thank them for returning all the items in good condition. Repeat Step 3, having children select a different toy to play with.

Follow-up:

1. Give each child some favorite item from the classroom. Tell children they are to pretend the item is theirs for the next 10 minutes. Children are to borrow items from each other to use during the next 10 minutes.

2. Select two volunteers to act out a situation in which one child returns a borrowed item which he or she has broken or damaged. The situation should include a dialogue between the child who borrowed the toy and the child from whom it was borrowed.

MY TEACHER'S THINGS

Purpose: To respect the property rights of others; to learn the proper way to ask for and return something which belongs to the teacher; to give adequate oral responses to questions.

Materials: Several common objects from the classroom that either belong to the teacher or are always kept in the teacher's desk (e.g. scissors, stapler, tape, felt-tip markers, ruler, pencil sharpener, paperweight, etc.)
Bell or a whistle
Large bag or a cardboard box

What To Do:

1. Gather the children together in a circle.

2. Place all of the objects in the bag or box and put the container in the center of the circle. Say, "Today we are going to play a game called My Teacher's Things. In my Surprise Box I have several things that are mine, and which I always keep in a special place. You will each have a turn to reach into the Surprise Box and take out one of my things."

3. Call on the first child to choose an object. When he/she has picked it out, ask the child to tell you what it is, what it is needed for, and where it belongs (or is) usually kept). Then ask, "If you needed to use it, how would you ask me if you could borrow it? . . . What would you do when you were finished using it?"

4. Discuss with the children the proper ways to ask for things and why they must be returned. Stress the point that the teacher's things must be handled carefully and kept in good condition because they are needed to do things for the entire class.

5. Let each child have a turn picking something out of the Surprise Box.

6. Allow children to use the "borrowed" item for 5-10 minutes. Tell them that when they hear the bell or whistle, they must return the item to you.

MY FAMILY'S THINGS

Purpose: To respect the property rights of others; to learn how to ask for and return an item that belongs to a family member.

Materials: Several common objects from the home that could belong to parents or siblings of the children (e.g. scissors, pots and pans, "dress-up" items, special toys, books, etc.)
Bell or a whistle
Large bag or a cardboard box

Several common objects from the home that could belong to parents or siblings of the children (e.g. scissors, pots and pans, "dress-up" items, special toys, books, etc.)
Bell or a whistle
Large bag or a cardboard box

What To Do:

1. Gather the children together in a circle.

2. Place all of the objects in a bag or box and put the container in the center of the circle. Say, "Today we are going to play a game called My Family's Things. In my Surprise Bag are several things that you might find in your home, but most of the time these things are put away because they belong to someone else. Each of you will have a chance to reach into my Surprise Bag and pull out one thing."

3. Call on one of the children to choose an object from the Surprise Bag. Once he/she has made a choice, ask questions like:
   —What is that?
   —What is it used for?
   —When do you use it?
   —Which member of your family would be most likely to own the (*item's name*)?
   —If you wanted to borrow it, how would you ask?
   —What would you do when you were finished playing with the ______?

MY FAMILY'S THINGS (continued)

4. Encourage a discussion with each of the children about proper ways to ask for things, and why they must be returned to their owners. Allow for differences in the children's responses, since each of their homes will be a little different.

5. Continue until all of the children have had a turn.

6. Allow children to play with the "borrowed" item for 5-10 minutes. Tell the children that when they hear the bell or whistle, they are to show you how they can carefully return the borrowed item to the Surprise Bag.

Follow-up:

1. Keep the Surprise Bag in a special area and allow the children to "borrow" items to play with during free play time. New items should be added periodically.

2. Tell each child to think of an item which they would like very much to borrow from a member of their family. Supply a sheet of note paper and an envelope for each child. Have each dictate a note to the family member whose possession he/she would like to borrow. The note should state why the child wants to borrow it, how he/she plans to use it, and promise to return it in good condition within a short period of time. Write the note which the child dictates, and address the envelope to the family member whom the child names. Have each child deliver the note. A day or two later, ask the children to report on the results of their written requests. Were they allowed to borrow the item? Did they handle it carefully? If they have already returned it, did they make sure it was still in good condition? How did their family feel about the responsible way in which they made their request?

Dear Bill,
Can I borrow your scout's manual? I want to show it to my class. I will bring it back soon.
love, Debby

BILLY THE BULLY

Purpose: To learn the importance of respecting others' property rights; to understand the feelings of someone whose property rights have been violated; to express ideas and opinions verbally.

Materials: Flannelboard
Flannelboard figures: Tommy, Billy the Bully, Sand Castle
(See Appendix 5)

What To Do:

1. With your flannelboard props handy, gather the children together and say, "I'm going to tell you a story about someone just like you."

2. Tell the following story (change Billy's name if there is a child by that name in group):

   "One day Tommy was playing in a sand pile in his back yard. (Put the flannelboard Tommy up.) Tommy loved to play in the sand, and he especially liked making great big sand castles. Tommy worked and worked, and finally he had a great big sand castle just like this one. (Put up the flannelboard sand castle.) Tommy was so proud of his sand castle that he sat back to admire it. All of a sudden he saw one of the boys from the neighborhood, Billy, coming toward him. (Put the flannelboard Billy up.) Well, do you know what Billy did? He ran right by the sand pile and kicked the castle with his foot. The sand went all over the place, and Tommy's beautiful sand castle just disappeared. (Tip sand castle over.)

   "Well, Tommy looked at what was left of his sand castle, and he was very, very sad. How would you boys and girls feel if somebody wrecked something that you had built? (Allow some time for discussion here.) Well, you can imagine how sad Tommy felt. He had spent a long time building his sand castle, and he didn't like Billy very much at all for what he had done.

   "Soon, some other children came over to play with Tommy. They started building houses and roads in the sand. After a while, Tommy forgot about how sad and angry he was at Billy. He was having fun playing with the other children.

BILLY THE BULLY (continued)

"Pretty soon, Billy came back again. He said to himself, 'Those boys and girls look like they are having fun. I think I'll go play with them.' Billy said, 'Can I play with you?'

"The boys and girls looked at each other. At one time or another, Billy had either taken something or wrecked something that belonged to each one of them. Nobody liked Billy the Bully very much.

"'You can't play with us, Billy,' said Tommy. 'You wrecked my sand castle and I don't like that. You have to stop wrecking things and taking things that don't belong to you.'

"'That's right, Billy; we're not going to play with you. You're nothing but a bully,' the other children said.

"So Billy just sat over on the side of the yard and watched the other boys and girls as they had fun playing in the sand."

3. Use the following questions to discuss the story, emphasizing the importance of respecting other children's property rights:
   - —How did Billy make Tommy feel angry and sad?
   - —Why do you think Billy knocked down Tommy's sand castle?
   - —Why don't the other boys and girls like Billy?
   - —Do you think the children are being fair by not letting Billy play with them?
   - —How do you think Billy feels when the other children won't let him play?
   - —Did Billy deserve to be treated that way? Why?
   - —Do you know any children who sometimes act like Billy?
   - —Do you ever act like Billy? How would your friends feel if you did?

4. End the lesson by discussing why it is wrong to interfere, wreck, hurt, knock down, or take things that other children own or are playing with. Emphasize that children who do such things often lose their friends and end up having no one to play with because nobody likes them.

BENNY BUNNY

Purpose: To pay attention to a story being told; to understand the importance of listening quietly and carefully to what others say.

Materials: "Benny Bunny" paper bag puppet (See Appendix 6)
Fox stick puppet
Small chair for a prop

What To Do:

1. Point to your ears and ask, "What are these? (Ears.) What do we use them for? (To hear, listen.) Close your eyes and listen for a moment." Pause for several seconds. "What did you hear? To be good listeners we must sit quietly without talking or making noises. We must not bother those next to us."

2. Hold up the Benny Bunny puppet. Say, "This is Benny Bunny. You would think that with such big ears he would be a good listener, but that hasn't always been so. When he was just a little bunny, he didn't listen very well at all. Let's use our ears to listen carefully to the story of Benny Bunny."

3. Read the following story:

   "Once upon a time there was a little bunny named Benny. (Hold up bunny puppet.) Benny lived with his mother in a house down a hole under a raspberry bush. (Hold puppet under chair.) Benny was usually a good little bunny; however, there were some times when he didn't listen and pay attention.

   "One day Benny's mother said, 'Benny, I'm going out to get some carrots. I'll be back in a few minutes. You stay in the house until I come back. I saw Freddy Fox near here yesterday, and he may still be around today.'

   "But Benny wasn't listening carefully to his mother. After she left, Benny felt like playing with his friend Sammy Skunk, who lived just a few trees away. So off he went!"

4. Stop and test comprehension by asking: "Where was Benny's mother? (Getting carrots.) When would she be back? (In a few minutes.) Where was Benny supposed to stay? (In the house.) Why? (Because Freddy Fox might be nearby.)

BENNY BUNNY (continued)

5. Continue story:

   "Just after Benny left his house, Freddy Fox jumped out of the bushes (Hold up Freddy Fox puppet) and began to chase Benny. Benny was very scared. He ran as fast as he could, through a briar patch and around the trees. Freddy was almost close enough to grab Benny by the tail when Benny found the hole under the raspberry bush that led to his house. In he jumped. Freddy could not follow because he was too big.

   "Benny sat down, shaking and crying. Suddenly he heard a voice say, 'Benny, what's wrong?' It was his mother, back with the carrots.

   "Benny looked up and said, 'Oh Mother, I was so scared! Freddy Fox almost caught me!'

   "Benny's mother said, 'Benny, if you had listened to me, you would not have left the house. Now stop crying, and let's have some carrots.'

   "'That sounds good to me,' said Benny. 'And from now on, I'm going to listen when someone says something to me.'"

6. Ask the following questions: "Did Benny always listen to his mother? What happened one day when Benny didn't listen? Why did Benny start to cry? Would Benny have gotten into trouble if he had listened? Why is it so important to listen and pay attention when someone, especially a parent, talks to you?"

Follow-up:

1. Ask for volunteers to role-play the story. Give them the stick puppet and the paper bag puppet to use.

2. Encourage children to use their imaginations to try and make up other stories about characters who did not listen, and who got into trouble because of it.

COUNT THE BIRDS

Purpose: To count the number of objects in a specified place; to participate appropriately in a group activity.

Materials: Flannelboard (or chalkboard)
Fence and birds for the flannelboard (Appendix 6)

Note: You need to cut out as many birds as your children can count. Use the pattern in Appendix 7.

What To Do:

1. Tell the children, "Today we are going to count! Let's see if we can count to ten together." Count slowly with the children. If they already know how to count beyond ten, let them continue up to twenty, if they can.

2. When you have finished counting together, say to the children, "Look at the flannelboard (chalkboard) and let's count the birds on the fence." Put ten birds up on the fence and point to each one as the children count them together.

3. Let each child come up and count the birds individually. If the child is able to count higher than ten, add more birds. If the child is not able to count to ten, lower the number of birds to his/her level.

4. Encourage the children to count higher by adding more birds. Don't raise the number so high that you frustrate the children, but use this lesson as an activity to teach math concepts.

5. Have a pair of children count alternately to ten (or higher). Child A: "One" . . . Child B: "Two" . . . A: "Three" . . . and so on. See if three children (or four) can do this.

Follow-up:

Use these flannelboard figures for addition and subtraction activities. Position a few birds on the fence and have some fly away from (subtraction) or fly to (addition) the fence.

APPENDIX

APPENDIX 1

To be used in conjunction with pages 92-93:	HAPPY OR SAD?
pages 94-95:	ANGRY FACES
pages 96-97:	HOW DID BOBBY FEEL?

APPENDIX 2
To be used in conjunction with page 98: HOW WOULD YOU FEEL?

APPENDIX 2
To be used in conjunction with page 98: HOW WOULD YOU FEEL?

APPENDIX 2
To be used in conjunction with page 98: HOW WOULD YOU FEEL?

APPENDIX 3
To be used in conjunction with page 100: SNACK TIME

APPENDIX 4
To be used in conjunction with pages 103-106: QUINCY RUNS AN ERRAND

APPENDIX 5
To be used in conjunction with page 112: BILLY THE BULLY

APPENDIX 6
To be used in conjunction with page 114: BENNY BUNNY

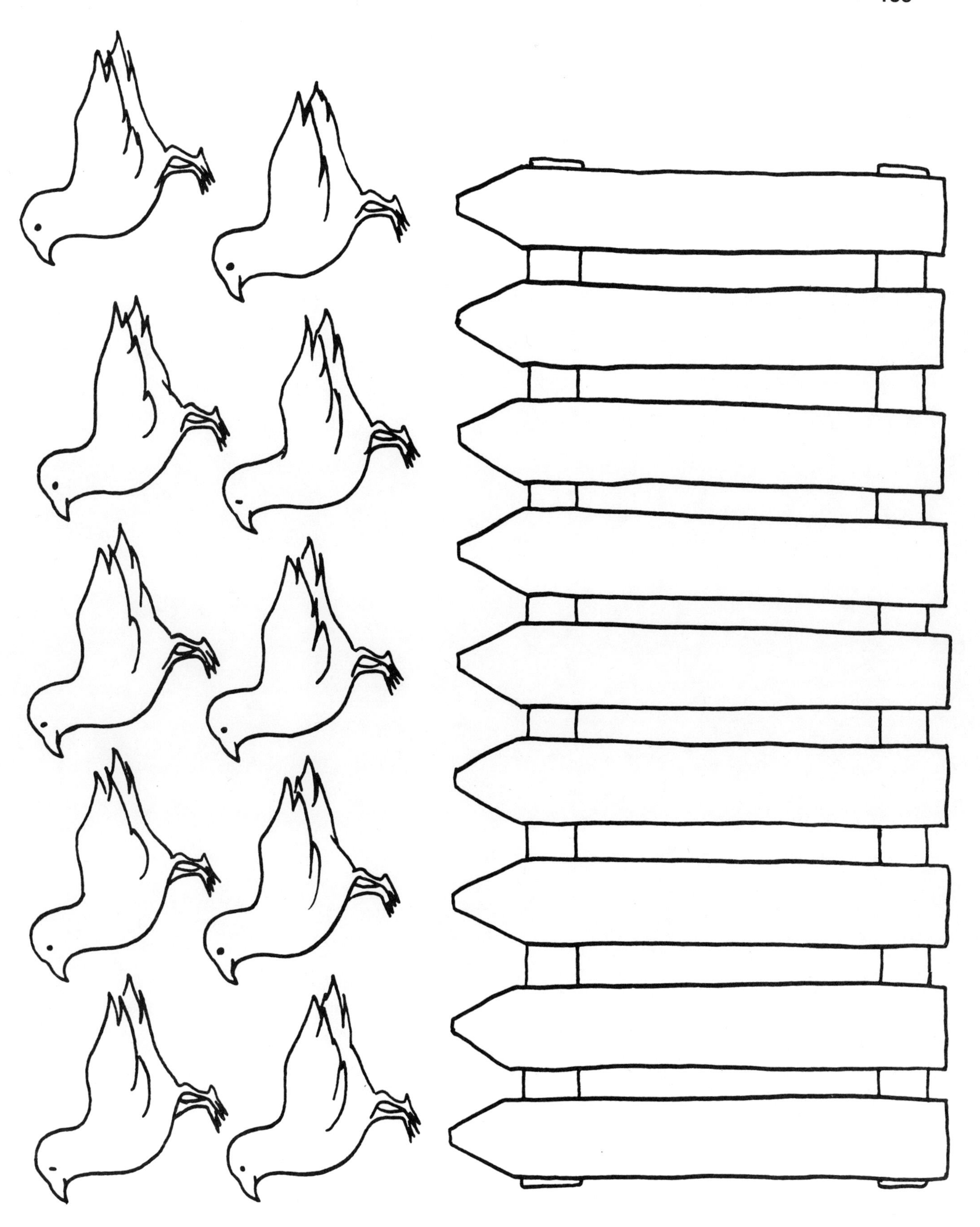

APPENDIX 7
To be used in conjunction with page 116: COUNT THE BIRDS